BEYOND the
CONGLOMERATES

Edward R. Bagley

BEYOND the CONGLOMERATES

The impact of the supercorporation
on the future of life and business

amacom

A DIVISION OF AMERICAN MANAGEMENT ASSOCIATIONS

Library of Congress Cataloging in Publication Data

Bagley, Edward R
  Beyond the conglomerates.

  Includes bibliographical references and index.
  1. Conglomerate corporations—United States.
I. Title.
HD2756.U5B28   338.8'042   74-4601
ISBN 0-8144-5369-4

First Printing

For Mother and Dad

PREFACE

THIS IS A FUTURIST BOOK. It predicts the rarest of events in the United States economy—the birth of two new kinds of huge corporations. The first is the supercorporation, which will be faster growing, much more diversified, tougher, and smarter than almost all of today's large corporations. I predict that from one to two dozen of these supercorporations will heave themselves into existence between the later 1970s and 1990.

The second new kind of corporation, of which I predict scores will emerge during this same period, is the semisupercorporation. The semisupers will be minor-league supercorporations, having most of the characteristics of true supers without quite reaching their extremely high standards. And there will be battalions of other large corporations emulating the supers, thereby adding much to the changes to be brought by the supers and semisupers.

The emergence of the handful of supercorporations and the more plentiful semisupers is likely to hit us harder than any other business happening in this century—for better or worse. If for better, these new kinds of corporations will be much more efficient and productive than nearly all of today's familiar types. The supers will be, for capable employees, far more stimulating, people-oriented places to work and grow in. Moreover, these entirely fresh corporations will actually help solve some of our groaning social problems. Thus, supercorporations and semisupers could—just could—be a new vehicle for making our tired system work.

But there is a dark side. The supercorporations, semisupers, and some of their emulators could turn out to be bigger bullies, worse polluters, and craftier opportunists than today's worst conventional corporations. Either way, you can ignore these new forms of corporate life about as easily as you can ignore the bulls when you cross their pasture.

You will find in this volume many specific predictions about the effects of these new kinds of corporations. You will also find futurist views of how to cut back, generically, the now unopposed growth of government bureaucracy; how to help deal with the grave capital starvation in the Third World; how to create wholly new U.S. cities profitably; how to engender within the corporate giants the same tenderness and concern shown by the best small businesses; and much more.

Most of the evidence in this futurist scenario comes from my own experience in looking at corporations from the inside out. Much of the remaining evidence has been assembled for you from current literature in economics and business, from thousands of items of corporate data, and from private research reports.

I have written this book because I believe that you, its readers, can have a measurable influence on the new supercorporations. Your first introduction to the supercorporations and semisupers will likely not be your last. May you heed this early warning, and may we all prepare ourselves better for this larger tide than we did for the coming of the adolescent conglomerates of the 1950s and 1960s. In other words, my wish is that this tour of your future be not so much entertaining as unforgettable.

I appreciate the advice and encouragement of Karl Detzer, roving editor of the *Reader's Digest,* and his knowledgeable wife, Clarice. Without their help, given in a memorable setting overlooking the Manitous, there might have been no book. I am also grateful to the staff members of AMACOM who contributed their talents and professionalism to the book.

EDWARD R. BAGLEY

CONTENTS

PART ONE

THE COMING
of the
SUPERCORPORATIONS

*For whatever deserves to exist deserves also to be
made known, for knowledge is the image of
existence and things mean and splendid exist
alike.*
                                        —FRANCIS BACON

Whether the predicted supercorporations and semisupers be mean
or splendid, we deserve to have early warning of their arrival in the
near future.

2,500 Years of Corporate Evolution

The changes necessary for the evolution of supercorporations can take place only if the legal framework and the historical acceptance of business corporations continue to survive. We precede our predictions, therefore, with a brief history of corporate survival to date, beginning with a flashback to the origins of the corporation.

The Romans of about 500 B.C. either absorbed a primitive concept of corporations from Greek commercial law or invented it themselves. One of the corporation's earliest features, still essential, is its legally supported continuity. Whereas a one-man business or a partnership must cease or reorganize whenever an owner dies, the corporation is empowered to go on for as many human generations as it can. The almost universal acceptance of the perpetual life of the corporation has fostered the practical development of today's corporate giants. Some of them literally make plans and enter into financial commitments for a hundred years from now.

Early in the eighteenth century, just before the dawn of the Industrial Revolution, came a discovery that helped make the corporation the overwhelming force it is today. In England, the idea of precisely limiting the financial liability of corporate stockholders was tried out. In the proprietorship and partnership forms of business, the owners were liable for all the debts of the business, even if paying them would strip the owners of all of their nonbusiness assets. This unlimited legal and financial liability continues in force today for noncorporate forms of business.

But in 1720, when the Englishman who invested £100 in the fabulous South Sea Bubble—a corporation—lost it all, he could not be sued for thousands more to help pay the staggering debts of the burst Bubble. This device of specifically limited financial liability, together with dreams of making fortunes, unlocked investors' hoards for many explorations and for the early industrialization that followed. Indeed, much of this discovery and industrialization could not have followed so rapidly without the financing made possible by the corporate form of enterprise.

Similarly, by the last third of the nineteenth century, the United States was on an even larger incorporation spree. This country's own industrial revolution and its population growth called for all the capital that could be coaxed from U.S. and foreign investors. Again, the limited liability of these investors was almost as important an inducement to invest as were the fortunes to be seized.

By the end of the last century and the beginning of this one, the apparently endless U.S. economic frontier had led to an immensely larger economy and to the first stage of its concentration in a few corporate hands. U.S. Steel, for example, became a giant overnight through the merging of a group of the then largest independent steelmakers. Mergers in other industries led to similar corporate concentrations, or trusts. These trusts, or huge corporations, soon became as boiling a public issue as pollution has been for us recently. Action followed. The first U.S. antitrust act, in 1890, led to the court-ordered breakup of John D. Rockefeller's Standard Oil trust by 1911.

The corporate form of enterprise has continued to be the flying wedge in the growth and dominance of our economy, now many times its $13.5 billion size in 1890, when trust-busting first became a national concern. Along the way, the twists and turns of corporate evolution have been pursued by encircling laws and public consensus. However, some students of the corporation, including Peter Drucker and Berle and Means, have felt that corporations regularly outrun the conscious intentions of both their corporate directors and the public.

This may well be true, in both the benefits that corporations have lavished on us and the geometrically growing problems that they have either fathered or not yet helped to resolve. So by the early post-World War II period, when our supercorporation story begins, the business corporation had reached a still higher pinnacle of concentrated power, effectiveness, and visibility. At that point—except for fears of a disastrous postwar depression—the corporate form of enterprise seemed positioned for still greater growth and impact on us all.

And so it was, until a strange thing began to happen. As we will see in the next three chapters, the typical corporation began to falter. The U.S. economy was growing at an unbelievable rate, a few growth companies were dazzlingly outperforming the economy, and some conglomerate corporations pranced in a brief imitation of these growth corporations; but in general, conventional corporations were not keeping up.

Now, after 2,500 years of glacial corporate evolution marked by the appearance of a few new kinds of corporations, I am predicting the emergence of two new kinds of corporations within the next five to fifteen years.

1

DISCOVERING the SUPERCORPORATIONS

THE FIRST POINT from which to scan the development of two new kinds of corporations is the fermenting scene in the United States. Never so wealthy, never so frustrated, we have been painting all kinds of bizarre pictures of our national future—or demise. These pictures are a part of the scenario in which our new types of corporations will develop.

The Future is Now

We are perched somewhere out beyond the end of our familiar world. We are told that we are "post-Christian" and "post-Renaissance" and are becoming "postindustrial."

With the death of our accustomed ways of life, we know that we face exploding perils: population explosion, self-propelled technology, vanishing resources, engulfing pollution, virulent nationalism, and an altogether mindless acceleration of problems over solutions.

Worst of all, our futurists disagree about whether there is even a chance for us to survive these perils. Thus, we do—or do not—have the means to sustain the lives of 14 billion people in the year 2070. We have—or have not—already passed the point of no return in polluting our planet. We can—or cannot—develop new resources and technology to prevent a universal depression from the exhaustion of natural resources. And so on.

One of the more compelling of the apocalyptic views is Robert Heilbroner's, who doubts that the expected end of economic growth will permit individual freedom to survive.[1] Confronting all this, I claim that there may be a ray of light partway down the tunnel, in the later 1970s and 1980s. Oddly enough, my modest futurist effort presumes to have some partial answers to the fermenting perils of this era. It is based on two fundamental predictions: first, two very new kinds of postindustrial corporations will be born—the supercorporation and the semisuper. They are going to collide head on with the best-selling perils of our time.

Second, these two new kinds of postindustrial corporations will either compound these perils or else tangibly help in handling them. It all depends on how we direct and control the new corporations. My futurist light partway down the tunnel, then, is the possibility that new forms of corporate life can lever us toward some relief and some solutions. We might thereby, in the already quaint words of William Faulkner, "not only survive, but prevail." (Note that for clarity I state my predictions in terms of what "will" happen. But you should substitute "probably will," for no futures can be guaranteed.)

My crystal ball clouds short of predicting whether these new postindustrial corporations will finally help or hurt us. I must leave this crucial determination to the reader's own predictions, and especially to his influence on the supercorporation and the semisuper.

THE VALUE OF THIS FUTURIST EFFORT

I have to believe that sometimes we can learn from the past and present, falteringly predict the future, and thereby prepare to tilt it in our favor. In a narrower corridor, consider that a forewarning might have led us to a quite different experience with conglomerates, and with ourselves, since the 1950s.

As I will remind you later in Part One, the conglomerates of the 1950s and 1960s were scandalously unsound. They invented earnings, they painted fairy-tale images, and they fooled the thousands of

---

[1] *An Inquiry Into the Human Prospect* (New York: Norton, 1974).

owners of businesses who sold out to them. They hornswoggled thousands of accountants, lawyers, and bureaucrats, as well as millions of investors. In addition to the human losses, the dollar losses were in the billions. Had we in the early 1950s had even a hazy forecast of what was afoot, it might never have happened that way at all.

So I am now offering several years' early warning, on a greater scale, about the evolution of still newer kinds of giant corporations, the supercorporations and the semisupers. There will be perhaps only one to two dozen supercorporations with uncommon power and influence. There will be scores of semisupers with much less individual clout; collectively, however, they may hit us as hard as the supercorporations themselves. These postindustrial corporations will plant themselves in our midst in the later 1970s and in the 1980s.

I believe that this kind of futurist effort is worth making, as an informed attempt to cope with the gross perils of the post-everything world. In fact, readers of this book can hardly justify a "future shock" reaction to supercorporations, given the explicitness of the predictions of their arrival.

MACROFUTURES VERSUS MICROFUTURES

A note on the distinction between this and other futurist works may help you sort out the many futures you are being offered at the bookstore.

Some of these forecasts are so macro—so broad and lofty—that they take far too little account of the specific, or micro, force of the U.S. corporation. Perhaps this omission creeps in because the corporation is as accustomed as our morning coffee. Others, alternatively, may perceive the corporation as a passive thing in the sweep of the really big picture.

In contrast, I will show you why I forecast greater—not less— influence and power for our largest business corporations; greater—not less—freedom, satisfaction, and income for most corporate employees; and a greater—not lesser—chance to prevail against our social perils, through the hyperpotent agency of the new supercorporations and their many emulators. The futurist Herman Kahn also concludes, in his compendium on corporations, that the postindustrial culture may not be postbusiness, because U.S. corporations are likely to enter areas traditionally considered the responsibility of government or the private individual.[2]

You may now begin to see the differences between the macrofutures that seem to require massive centralized control for our own good and the microfuture of the new supercorporations and their followers. In microforce, millions of people and hundreds of billions of dollars in resources will be taking small and unglamorous bites out of the problems. They can contribute, however haltingly, to a lively and less restrictive postindustrial society until about 1990.

Some Definitions and Descriptions

Before discussing the three historical forces that are forming the supercorporations, let us first define these new corporations, along with the other corporate types with which we will be dealing.

Supercorporations. The full-fledged supercorporation will have four hallmarks: (1) at least one billion dollars in size; (2) growth at an average of 10 percent annually, equal to about twice the average rate; (3) extensive diversification into at least three disparate industries; and (4) a rare degree of resourcefulness, flexibility, aggressiveness, and creativity. In addition to meeting these essentials, supercorporations will usually, but not necessarily, be multinational in scope. Let us take a closer look at each of the four requirements.

Supercorporations will be very large, with sales or assets of at least a billion dollars. A number of them will be in the multi-billion-dollar class, and a few will have sales or assets of $20 billion or more.

Supercorporations will also grow, consistently, about twice as fast as the average corporation—at an average rate of 10 percent per year. Peter Drucker has suggested that it is arithmetically and practicably impossible for large corporations to grow at this super rate. He may be right for the long-term future. However, within the next 15 years, there is a strong basis—a strong impulse—for a special handful of big corporations to attain this "impossible" rate. Actually, a few companies have already done so in the past 15 years, with conditions less promising for their super growth.

Supercorporations will be extensively, almost wildly, diversified

---

[2] *The Future of the Corporation* (New York: Mason & Lipscomb, 1974).

into three or more different industries. This diversification, as we will see, smacks of the gyrations of the conglomerate corporations of the 1960s. In the case of the supercorporations, however, the extensive diversification will typically move into a smaller number of fields. Furthermore, this diversification will be founded upon strategic plans and on cadres of line and staff management, which the conglomerates of the last two decades could only try to claim in their slick-paper, four-color annual reports. Thus, the great diversification that helped founder the conglomerate corporations will be tempered to a less brittle range of large-scale supercorporation ventures.

Less easy to describe, the supercorporations will be far more resourceful, flexible, aggressive, and creative than the usual kinds of corporations. Part Two of this book will present a series of concrete examples of the managerial concepts and methods that some large corporations will adopt and that will enable them to become supercorporations. These concepts and methods include, for instance, new forms of organizational structure, a new way of creating entrepreneurial force, and, especially, improved means of managing people.

Corporations with these characteristics will obviously be far superior to nearly all other large corporations in our history and will indeed be "super." They will come into being as the offspring of two very different types of today's corporations. Parent No. 1 will be the typical large, mature corporation, such as Chrysler, Bethlehem Steel, American Can, Goodyear, St. Regis Paper, Allied Chemical, Georgia-Pacific, Standard Brands, and Allis-Chalmers. Note carefully that most of these present-day giants will not actually become supercorporations. Rather, within their category ("conventional corporations," defined below) there will be a few that will become bases for supercorporations.

Parent No. 2 of the new supercorporations will be the best concepts and practices to survive the wreckage of the conglomerates of the 1960s. To emphasize: this second parent will not be the body of a 1960 conglomerate but the aggregate of the best ideas, methods, and experience of such companies. Some of the essential parental strains from the conglomerate side will be broader diversification, a thirst for faster growth, more flexible organization and operation, and more productive use of capital.

With this unique set of bloodlines, it is clear that the supercorporation will be a different kind of corporate being, not simply a larger version of the same old thing. At least a few present-day companies already seem to foreshadow the supercorporations of tomorrow. General Electric and ITT are two companies which might someday give birth to such supercorporations.

Semisupercorporations. One of the biggest fallouts of the supercorporations will be their extreme influence on thousands of other corporations. Narrowly, I predict that there will also arise scores of semisupercorporations. These semisupers will have most of the characteristics of supercorporations, but will fall short in important respects. For example, a corporation that is both large and diversified enough may not be able to grow more than, say, 8 percent per year in earnings per share. This would still be an extraordinary company. It would be seen as influenced deeply by supercorporations and similar to them. This semisuper is the second new kind of corporation of the near future.

"Infected" corporations. Yet another concentric wave of influence of the forthcoming supercorporations will wash against thousands of other U.S. corporations. These, which cannot become supercorporations or even semisupers, will still be infected with some of the ideas and methods that will prove so hugely powerful for the supercorporations. I also refer to these infected corporations as emulators of the supers.

One of the things I cannot predict is which group of corporations—the supers, the more plentiful semisupers, or the far more numerous "infected" corporations—will have the greatest impact on business and society. Arguments can be made for any of these three possibilities. But wherever the greatest influence comes from, that influence will be felt first on the familiar kinds of corporations and then in our society generally. These more familiar kinds of corporations have been mentioned before; let us now define and describe them.

Conventional corporations. These are the companies we usually think of as normal, large corporations. Some of them were named above as possible parents of the future supercorporations. Other conventional corporations are Anderson Clayton, Zenith Radio, Amax, Time Inc., Northrop, Essex International, and ARA Services. Most banks, financial companies, retailers, utilities, and transportation companies are also conventional corporations, by our lights.

As compared with supercorporations, conventional corporations are (1) slower growing, with average annual rates of about 5 percent as against the predicted 10 percent for the supers; (2) less extremely diversified, operating in one industry or in several related fields, as Colgate-Palmolive does in the related fields of household products, toiletries, drugs, and health-care products; and, again not as tangibly, (3) less change-oriented, possessing lesser degrees of the resourcefulness, flexibility, aggressiveness, and creativity that are principal requirements for the supercorporation. In other words, the conventional corporation is managing itself and its people much the same as it did 20 to 30 years ago. Beneath an overlay of administrative fads and fashions, the conventional corporation will chalk up noticeably less net improvement than the supercorporation.

It should be reemphasized that neither size nor multinational scope determines a corporation's status as conventional, semisuper, or super. Many conventional corporations are small; a few will be larger than some of the supers. Likewise, some conventional corporations, such as Coca-Cola, are multinational, but this alone does not make them supercorporations.

"Swinging" conglomerates. During the 1960s, Litton Industries, Gulf + Western, Ling-Temco-Vought, Whittaker, Boise Cascade, and a few dozen other corporations seemed to be acquiring another company every week, and a few did just that, for a while. They also seemed to break—successfully—every rule in the book, and seemed to be growing faster than almost every other company.

One of the principal family characteristics of these "swinging" conglomerates was their high price-earnings multiples during the 1960s. These multiples ranged from 30 to 70, while most conventional corporations had price-earnings multiples of 25 or less. (Since the depressed stock markets of 1973 and 1974, most conventional corporations have had price-earnings multiples of 15 or less. The Dow Jones Industrial Average, mainly composed of conventional corporations, registered a low price-earnings multiple of 10 or less during this depressed-market period.)

On the other hand, the conglomerate corporations' market valuations, which lasted up to ten years for some of the swingers, indicated that their earnings were worth, in cold cash, 300 percent to over 500 percent more than the earnings of such very solid conventional corporations as General Motors or AT&T.

There were, and are, some other, less flamboyant conglomerates that never snared the astronomical price-earnings multiples of the swingers—for example, Tenneco, W. R. Grace, IU International Corp., ITT, Textron, and Ogden. These less seductive conglomerates were also large, and more solid than nearly every swinger, but they did not, and do not, have the incredible impact on the public and business mind that the swingers once had.

Growth companies. According to securities people, there must have been thousands of "growth" companies at one time or another since World War II. A few of these fulfilled the promises and are now household words—IBM, Xerox, and Eastman Kodak, for example. These few growth companies are the true stars of the free-market system and are the rarest of the types of corporations discussed here. The frantic attempt to duplicate the records of these growth companies heightened the attractiveness, for a while, of the swinging conglomerates.

Turnarounds. Some large corporations, such as Esmark, Inc. (formerly Swift & Co.), have a run of bad years, and then a new management comes in and begins the rebuilding. The Wall Street expression for this situation is "turnaround." We are not greatly interested in turnarounds relative to the evolution of supercorporations, but it is useful to distinguish the turnarounds from growth companies. The former can look like the latter for a few years, while the fat is being squeezed out, but turnarounds do not typically become leading growth companies, and few, if any, turnarounds are likely to become supercorporations.

There you have the cast of characters for the futurist play of corporations: the fast-growing, large, diversified, brilliantly managed, and sometimes multinational supercorporations; the semisupers, which are also-rans compared to supers but winners by any other standard; the conventional corporations, which are of any size, but are slower growing, less extremely diversified, and less superbly managed than the supers and the semisupers; the swinging conglomerates of the 1960s, which were raffishly diversified, instantly acquisitive, and cleverly manipulative for a while, and were the sometime darlings of the stock market, with the highest price-earnings multiples in living memory; the too few growth companies, such as IBM, which so many try to copy; and the turnarounds, which may look like growth companies or supercorporations in the early stages of rebuilding from the depths.

Now we are prepared to turn to the three historical forces whose action on some of today's large conventional corporations is right now converting them into the supercorporations and semisupercorporations of tomorrow.

Three Forces Producing Supercorporations

As you explore for the first time the idea of supercorporations, you will probably be struck by the masses of previously overlooked evidence that some of our large corporations are changing greatly, a few of them so much so that they are already becoming supers. You may agree with me that such enormously significant evolutions from familiar corporate types could not have been hammered out merely by the ambitions of a few overachieving executives. In fact, the three determinative forces we are about to explore are laying a new economic framework within which a few of these overachievers can build beyond their fondest dreams in a conventional yesterday.

The three major forces leading to the formation of supercorporations and semisupers are (1) the unslaked urge to grow; (2) the disappointing and faltering post-World War II performance of many conventional corporations; and (3) the promise, followed by the disasters, of most of the 1960 conglomerates.

Seen in perspective for probably the first time, these three combined forces are creating in today's performance vacuum an enormous opportunity for further and faster corporate growth by a few gifted management groups. A review of these historical determinants is the starting point for discovering the emerging supercorporations and semisupers.

THE UNSLAKED URGE TO GROW

Two of the historical forces that will bring the supercorporations into being are recent, affecting us only since World War II. The first historical determinant of the supers, however, has been always with us in some form: the primordial urge for living things to grow or multiply. Biologists and others point out that most forms of life reach a state of equilibrium within themselves and with their environments and may thereafter add little, if anything, to their physical size, their propensities, or their numbers. They may also decline or disappear.

In a similar vein, Sir Stafford Beers [3] raises the challenge of whether the organic nature and structure of the business corporation can physically survive any further expansion. His argument, which points to compelling parallels between the living organism and the corporate organism, is tempting, especially to the many people who have an innate dread of monstrously large corporations getting ever larger.

I must take the opposite view. For one thing, we observe that some man-made structures, such as the business corporation, seem not yet to have reached an internal limit to their structural or functional growth. For example, the Bank of America looks to be as sound and growth-oriented now, with deposits of over $43 billion, as it was when it was one forty-third as large and building toward 43 times its size.

Another thing: our postindustrial environment is technologically ordered on such a gargantuan scale that we do not fully understand or control it. However, we do know that sealing wax and buggy whips are not enough. Neither are minicomputers, portable plants for industrial gases, and other small artifacts. And we are gearing our postindustrial world to ever higher levels of capability and complexity. These new levels cannot be conceived, financed, built, or operated by smaller corporate structures alone.

To take the developed world's petroleum situation as an example, there is no way for small companies to get and ship the oil and gas they need. None. Later, I refer to supertankers, which cost over $100 million now and will cost more in the future. They are contracted for in groups: one supertanker amounts to almost nothing. On the other hand, no small corporation could handle even one supertanker. Add numbers of supertankers to numbers of refineries, pipelines, distribution systems, research complexes, and so on and you have an indication of my answer to the organic challenge.

There are two other liberating views of the charge that large corporations cannot or should not become still larger. The first is a central conclusion of Peter Drucker, that management is one of the few success stories of the century.[4] He considers management a success as a new discipline, a new function, and a new leadership group. He has indicated no finite limit—no organic limit—to the size of corporate organizations that can be managed, provided that the economic and other aspects are secured. I add that the further evolution of management

---

[3] *Brain of the Firm* (London: Allen Lane, Penguin Press, 1972).
[4] *Management: Tasks, Responsibilities, Practices* (New York: Harper & Row, 1974).

will continue to make feasible those larger corporations that embody economic necessity and social acceptability.

The second view is frightening. One of my grave concerns is the decline in research and development in the United States. The federal government's R&D spending has declined in constant dollars, and industry has barely held its own. Dr. William O. Baker, president of Bell Telephone Laboratories, points out that at least six of the best laboratories in the country were closed down in one year—1971— including the Shell Oil Fundamental Research Laboratories of Emoryville, California.[5] He also reports that the course of patenting and inventing in the United States (and other countries) is down. Again, this is not only a future problem, it is a problem now. Although Dr. Baker believes that medium-size and smaller companies should play a major part in expanding R&D, I take the view that certain tasks require the financial, technical, and managerial support of the largest companies. It was, of course, Bell Labs itself that invented the whole domain of solid state electronics.

The answer to the organic challenge, then, is that if very large corporations did not exist, we would have to invent them and hang onto them. If they were undesirable as business corporations, they could be invented as government corporations, as in the case of ENI, the Italian state energy corporation. Moreover, they would unavoidably be very close in design to the imperfect creatures of today. They would have to be staffed by imperfect people, which would lead us back to the organic and other corporate shortcomings with which we now live. The necessary corporations, if we did not have them, would not only have to be created as multi-billion-dollar entities—that is plain. But— and this may give Sir Stafford and others real pause—the necessary postindustrial corporations would—and will—have to be organically and functionally capable of *doubling or trebling their present multi-billion-dollar size within this century.*

So the proposition is really reversed in the microfuture of the postindustrial corporation. The question is not whether existing conventional corporations are too large and organically unsound and whether they will wither away. Rather, the question at the core of our survival is: Can corporations, whether controlled by business, the government, or a combination of the two, effectively double or treble their already

---

[5] *Forbes* (February 15, 1974), pp. 67–71.

enormous size in order merely to keep up with our complex needs for survival?

Can they grow to transform geothermal, plasma, solar, coal gasification and liquefaction, and other high-technology energy sources from Sunday supplement stories to delivered BTUs? Can the very largest corporations be developed to help cope with horrors only now imagined? The Italian systems analyst Roberto Vacca, in *The Coming Dark Age*,[6] predicts the total collapse of our technological systems no later than 1994. Not just energy, but transportation, communications, and everything else. Certainly the most valiant small and medium-size corporations are not staffed to do as much as address such worldwide problems. Can the supers and other very large corporations help?

My new, provisional answer is that they can. Though fault-ridden, supers and semisupers will have the organic structure; they will have the stamina, staff, systems, capital, motivation, the anatomy and physiology, and the other needed factors. They will help to serve us as we must be served, in a world that will not shrink to fit the conceptions of inherently limited corporate size.

The U.S. economy is another human structure that seems to have displayed no absolute, innate limit to its growth. Actually, some economists are saying, on the contrary, that our economy may be the first in all history to be permanently self-generating, something like a nuclear breeder reactor. At any rate, the ultimate potentials of the probably continuing force of economic and corporate growth do not yet seem to be internally circumscribed.

This so far irresistible force for growth in the U.S. economy and business community has called forth such predictions as a $2.75 trillion economy by 1985, with even more growth expected to mushroom reliably thereafter. Evidently, the postindustrial corporations are not "postgrowth," but will be part of a reciprocal growth relationship with the economy as a whole.

We can say that, regardless of the causes of this first historical force toward the formation of giant supercorporations, economic and business growth is here and can safely be expected to remain with us, at whatever future rate of gain. The second and third forces have been negative, in that both conventional corporations and conglomerates

---

[6] Garden City, N.Y.: Doubleday, 1974.

have failed to seize fully the gains available to them from the extraordinary growth in our economy. There is a compelling urge for something else to fill the performance vacuum, and that something else is the supercorporation, together with its little brother, the semisuper.

SHOULD WE CANCEL OUR GROWTH?

Before dealing with the limitations of the conventional and conglomerate corporate forms, a contemporary challenge to economic growth must first be dispatched. We must all take a position on the pleas or warnings that economic growth, if not purposely abated, may kill all life on our planet. A catchphrase of both popular and high governmental sources is "affluence breeds effluents."

From sources as different as Sicco L. Mansholt and the James G. Blaine Society comes a challenge to the value and the acceptability of economic growth, a challenge not even a part of science fiction ten to fifteen years ago. Sicco L. Mansholt, president of the Commission of the European Communities, has been called by some Europe's No. 1 bureaucrat. He warns that economic growth may not be compatible with a livable environment and urges that steps be taken to curb any economic growth that is detrimental to the environment.

The James G. Blaine Society is a group of Oregonians who have made the television news shows and the wire services by asking people not to move to Oregon. "The mosquito is the state bird" is one of their typical sallies. Whether this group is serious or not, the state of Oregon is deadly so. Its governor, Thomas L. McCall, has kept new fossil-fuel plants out of the state—entirely. The actions of the government of Oregon and hundreds of other governments are a direct challenge to growth, a challenge that is not only conceptual but practical. If some opinion leaders merely debate the net social profit from unthinking growth, that is one thing. But if the enforced regulations of most governments drive costs up, profits down, and growth out, that is a horse of another color.

Reaction, as we know, set in by 1972. Those who think that a growing economy and corporate world, properly channeled, are primary agents for reducing environmental pollution have found voices. The book *The Retreat From Riches,* by Peter Passell and Leonard Ross, for example, argues both that economic growth is essential for our general well-being and that some degree of pollution control should be subsidiary to economic growth—not the reverse.[7] Counterattacking on another front, the British physicist John Maddox, in his book *The Doomsday Syndrome,* has struck out against some of the underlying contentions and data of environmentalists.[8] Wherever the truth may lie, the erratic pendulum of opinion has started to swing back from total environmental priority to a growth-with-improved-environment mix that has yet to be defined.

We can conclude that economic growth will remain at least as high a priority as environmental improvement. The question of whether this should be so is left to others. In any case, by reinforcing the acceptability of further economic growth, we reaffirm economic and business growth as a historical determinant of the coming of the supercorporations and semisupers.

Some Additional Aspects of Economic Growth

Two other aspects of our economic growth mold its historical force as a contributor to the evolution of the supercorporation. One aspect is the preeminence of private-sector growth, and the other is the continuing predominance of large corporations in our economic growth. In the U.S. economy, after an all-time record increase in governmental expenditures at all levels, the private sector overshadows the public sector. In our gross national product of more than a trillion dollars, private business accounts directly for about two-thirds. Or, as Calvin Coolidge said it nonstatistically in 1925, "The business of America is business."

Another patent feature of our economic growth that is helpful to our study of supercorporations is that much of it in the private sector has been registered through large corporations as a group. Thomas Jefferson's nation of farmers and small merchants died not many decades after he did. The 500 largest industrial corporations in the 1974 *Fortune* directory accounted for 65 percent of the sales of all U.S. industrial companies, as well as 79 percent of their total profits and 76 percent of all their employees. That is, only 0.0003 percent of some 1,700,000 U.S. corporations account for about three-quarters of the

---

[7] New York: Viking, 1973.
[8] New York: McGraw-Hill, 1973.

mass of all industry. Large concentrations exist also in banking, finance, transportation, utilities, and retailing.

A Deep Bow to Small Business

This is a good place to put in perspective my attitude toward small business relative to my discovery of two new classes of huge corporations to be added to our business population.

My tribute to the economic and social values of small business applies to all small businesses. We know that most small companies—the office machine repairman, the fuel oil distributor, the parts manufacturer, the neighborhood delicatessen, the noncorporate farmer, the car dealer, the manufacturer's sales agent, most home builders, and so many others—will remain small. The unglamorous, small-growth small business is as essential to the expected supercorporations as it is to other large customers. Without the products and services of the very smalls, the bigs just could not function as we now know them.

I also have a warm feeling for those occasional small businesses that skyrocket into bigness. Horatio Alger is not dead, nor even out of fashion. His crew is still doing extraordinary things, as the examples below will confirm.

The values traditionally imputed to the traits of both growth and nongrowth small business are likely to endure, especially in the world of ever larger corporations. Quick response and adaptation to the market, mobility, and the ability to innovate in some areas—traits natural to small companies—are of great value and should enable small businesses to survive as long as do large corporations. The social and human values of such traits as independence, greater attention to and accommodation of the individual, and often deep roots in their communities make small businessmen a desired part of our economy and society for all time.

In even the narrowest business terms, small businesses have been leaders in an astounding array of products, services, and business practices. As we will see later in Part One, most of the 1960 conglomerates began as small businesses, although this is not generally realized. Beyond this singular occurrence, small businesses have made the following contributions, to name only a smattering of them:

Microwave Associates, Inc., with annual sales in the $10 million range, is taking business away from AT&T, which, with annual sales of $10.6 billion, is 600 times larger. Microwave Associates, starting at zero in 1950, was formed to produce components for radar and communications systems. Now the company has won contracts to build and operate new common-carrier networks in New England and in four South Atlantic states for the three major broadcasting networks. The networks are switching from AT&T, which until now has had 90 percent of their business.

You would hardly call a $100 million per year business a small one, yet Stratford of Texas Inc. is our second example of the occasional small business that gets large. Started from scratch as recently as 1970 by Robert Gow, the company is ingeniously automating and rationalizing agricultural production. So far, Stratford is fattening cattle for 3¢ to 4¢ per pound below the national average, and is equally clever in its chicken and potted plants divisions.

A third example of a company that we forget was recently small is MGIC Investment Corp. of Milwaukee. Max H. Karl began "Magic," as it is called, in 1956.. He had difficulty in raising the needed $250,000 of initial capital. His barber, one of the early investors, put in $2,000. The company was formed to insure home mortgages more flexibly and less expensively than the federal government's FHA. In the first month, MGIC insured just four mortgages, but the idea proved so attractive that the company now insures up to 25,000 mortgages per month.

The company has since expanded into insuring mortgages on commercial buildings and on mobile homes, and has also gone into construction financing, home building, and operating the first nongovernmental secondary market for mortgages. Along the way, MGIC has broadened the entire market for mortgage insurance, and has pioneered in insurance for both the principal and interest on municipal bonds and on subordinated debentures issued by savings and loan associations.

All this adds up to 1973 gross revenues of $170 million, with net profits of $27.7 million. Pretty good for a small business that took in less than a quarter of a million dollars in its first year. Pretty good, too, for the founder's barber, whose $2,000 investment has been worth over $2 million.

In addition to these three big growth records from small businesses, others in the recent past have pioneered these new fields:

CATV; snowmobiles, pleasure boats, and several other types of recreational vehicles; and ethnic foods. In the more distant past, some fields that were developed largely by small businesses were automobiles, aircraft and airlines, industrial maintenance and sanitation supplies, wholesale and retail establishments, textiles, furniture, and drug, toiletry, and cosmetic products.

Although there are natural competitive and other conflicts between large and small business, we should not expect the advent of supercorporations to hurt small business across the board. Part Two, dealing with the effects of the supers on businesses and business people, points out that supers are likely to be better customers, suppliers, and competitors than most other large corporations. Some small businesses—along with some large ones—will suffer from the smarter and tougher policies and decisions of the supers, but others will gain by them. On balance, if supercorporations behave as astutely as they are supposed to, they will promote a healthy and demanding business environment for small business—and the supers will expect the continuing survival and prosperity of small business. Even more, the exceptionally astute management of the supercorporations would recognize the life-giving contributions of small business, rather than passing off small business as a distraction.

One more point of perspective on small business is needed relative to our loud concern about social problems. After allowing for the invaluable nature of small business, we must admit that its smallness inhibits many meaningful contributions to old and new social concerns. For instance, the smallest of small businesses are not required to support or comply with programs ranging from unemployment compensation to occupational safety and health. The Ohio Chamber of Commerce has given me a list of seven of the socially motivated requirements from which the smallest businesses are exempt (figures in parentheses are the minimum number of employees required before a company must comply): unemployment compensation (2), employer payment of applicant's physical examination fee (3), discriminatory employment practices (4), required semimonthly payment of wages (5), Occupational Safety and Health Act (8), prohibition against discrimination in wages because of sex (10), voluntary arbitration of industrial disputes (25). Although we are dealing with the smallest of businesses, they account for the largest number of all businesses.

On a larger scale, some of the socially related efforts by business, such as hiring the hard-core unemployed, have been underwritten principally by large corporations.

With deep, enduring gratitude to the brave spirit and tenacity of the U.S. small businessman and his sometimes long-suffering family, we return to the historical trends and forces leading to the emergence of the supercorporations and the semisupers. The first such force, as we have just seen, is the unslaked urge to grow. The second is the faltering record of the postwar conventional corporation in the face of unparalleled growth opportunities.

2

THE FALTERING
CONVENTIONAL CORPORATIONS

IN ADDITION to the ever present underlying growth impetus, a more recent historical force in the development of supercorporations is the disappointing growth of many large conventional corporations. Right after World War II, these firms started with a bang, as they went about satisfying pent-up demand. Their growth, however, ended with a whimper: near the end of the postwar period, they scarcely kept pace with the rate of inflation.

The Disappointing Growth Record

Despite its imperfections, I have adopted growth in earnings per share over a sustained period of five to ten years or more as the most useful measure of corporate growth. Thus, unless otherwise indicated, we will be talking in terms of average annual compounded growth in earnings per common share of the companies involved.

The first of our indicators of disappointingly modest corporate growth is the aggregate trend of corporate profits. On an economywide and long-term basis, earnings have declined persistently, through or around recessions and booms. In 1950, after-tax profits of all manufacturing corporations were 7.1 percent of sales; by 1966, profits were down to 5.6 percent of sales; by 1971, down again to 4.2 percent of sales. Moreover, total dollar profits for all U.S. corporations were less, absolutely, in 1971 than in 1966. At the same time, the gross national product increased 39.6 percent, and employee compensation in industry increased 42.1 percent. The corresponding data on profits were probably worse for the conventional corporations, for the data given above include the buoyant effects of growth companies like IBM and some of the apparent growth of the conglomerates. By another measure, corporate profits fell from 16 percent of national income in 1950 to 10 percent in 1972. The economywide decrease in corporate earnings makes the growth company especially rare, and especially interesting as a model for the corporate executive. We know that most companies cannot be growth companies, just as most entrants lose in every race. Still, the lure of winning is there, and in the corporate race, the few winners of the growth prize are well rewarded indeed.

The growth problem is also registered in the aggregate financial statements of large corporations. Their data are incomplete and partly conflicting, but two useful sources of information on the relatively slow average growth of corporate profits are the *Fortune* annual directories of the largest U.S. corporations and the *Forbes* annual reports on American industry. These two sources are statistically different, yet they point in the same unsatisfactory direction.

According to *Fortune*'s figures, which are based on ten-year periods, the median rate of growth of the 500 largest U.S. industrials during the years 1955–1973 has been only about 6 percent to under 10 percent per year. This growth rate was typically logy, relative to that of growth companies and conglomerates. However, the growth rate of large corporations got a big boost in 1973, with an extraordinary 39 percent increase over 1972.

Even these record-breaking results could only increase the ten-year 1963–1973 median growth rate to 9.73 percent. This was the highest in the history of the *Fortune* studies, and was an exception for several reasons. First, the 1973 growth rate, and its effect on the ten-year median growth rate, were bloated by record-breaking inflation. Another key factor is that 1973 was just one year, whereas the essence of the supercorporation growth requirement is a sustained rise in average earnings per share over a period of five to ten years or more. And we must note again that all years' growth rates are overstated for conventional corporations by the extreme results of growth companies, and the results reported by conglomerates.

On balance it appears that the long-term average growth in earnings per share of conventional corporations was in the order of 5 percent per year. This makes a strong contrast with the 10 percent rate required for the predicted supers.

Forbes has used somewhat different calculations of corporate growth for over 700 large U.S. corporations and has worked with five-year periods. The *Forbes* results also show relatively low growth rates for the latter part of the postwar period: for the years 1966–1971 the median growth rate for these corporations was 1.2 percent; for 1967–1972 it was 3.6 percent. Both sources include the "growth" effects of inflation. If adjusted to offset inflation, the growth rates of large U.S. corporations would be substantially lower. Less than 37% of the *Forbes*-surveyed companies recorded average earnings gains in 1968–1973 that were large enough to offset the 1973 inflation rate of 7.5 percent. Also, something like 20 percent of all U.S. industry profits for 1973 and 1974 were coming from paper profits on inventories—not from company operations.

Another discouraging calculation of corporate profits and inflation is supplied by economist George Terborgh in the *Financial Analysts Journal* for June 1974. Nonfinancial corporations in 1973 reported pretax profits of $96.5 billion, but Terborgh figured they were overstated by more than $26 billion because inflation caused an understatement of both depreciation and the costs of inventory. Adjusting both 1973 profits and 1965 profits by the same method, the 1973 profits become less than two-thirds of the 1965 profits.

A third set of figures that indicates a less than satisfying rate of growth by large U.S. corporations is the inconsistent and short-term results reported by many corporations. Wall Street's classic query, "What have you done for me lately?" is practical as well as cynical.

Reeves Bros. Inc., AMK, Mattel, and Revlon, if you recall them, were among the leaders in the growth lists of less than ten years ago. Chrysler, admittedly in a cyclical industry, showed an 18.7 percent average annual growth in earnings per share in the *Fortune* Directory for 1961–1971, but *Forbes* showed Chrysler with a 7.4 percent decline for the five-year period 1967–1972. Eastman Kodak, one of the most widely held institutional favorites and an outstanding company by any measure, registered only a 6.3 percent average growth rate in the *Forbes* report for 1967–1972. Raytheon, now well diversified from its earlier dependence on defense contracting, showed an impressive 11.8 percent average rate of growth in 1961–1971, but only 5.1 percent in

1967–1972. Olin, FMC, and General Dynamics were once stars, and Anaconda a blue chip. Many of the august names in Wall Street are either gone or showing poorer earnings performance than most of their clients.

Reasons for the Waning Growth

Many conventional corporations actually had self-imposed internal constrictions on their growth. Ironically, these were commonly viewed as good business and sound policy, and even as common sense. The constricting elements were prudent operating policy, prudent financial policy, and consensual constraints, or "the rules of the game." These concepts are sensible enough, but in practice they were overapplied.

PRUDENT OPERATING POLICY

The first overapplication was in what has been called prudent operating policy. For example, a typical top management and board of directors policy required that the conventional corporation stick to its last, as it was frequently voiced. Another prudent policy of such a corporation was to maintain 100 percent control of every business or profit center in which it was involved. Other common features of prudent operating policy were not acquiring very many companies, cautious and conservative compensation of key men, avoiding entrenched competition, and so on. The first two examples will be used to convey the whole point of the prudent operating policy syndrome that governed most conventional corporations.

Sticking to one's last, as the shoemaker sticks to his last, meant that the conventional corporation stayed within, or comfortably close to, its existing industries, fields, product lines, or services. A railroad was a railroad and not a transportation company. The maker of tetraethyl lead for premium gasolines was not a chemicals company. A metals company, dependent for generations on foreign ores, was just that. A banana company was a banana company, not a foods company. The major aerospace contractor was only that and had better not gamble away his basic business by going as far afield as airborne electronics or commercial aircraft.

The results of such a policy can be seen clearly if we compare the excellent growth of the Union Pacific Railroad with the bankruptcy of the New York, New Haven & Hartford and other railroads. After adjustments for the innumerable differences in route structure and so on, Union Pacific's record, especially as compared to that of the other railroads, shows profitable growth, with nearly one-third of its increasing profits in oil, real estate, and other nonrail enterprises.

Then there is the difference between Republic Aviation Corp. and McDonnell Douglas. Republic was one of the largest manufacturers of military aircraft during World War II and the Korean War. Less than ten years after Korea, Republic's remains were swept into Fairchild Industries Inc. McDonnell was also a nondiversified defense contractor. It took over the ailing Douglas and got a tenable hold on the commercial aircraft market. McDonnell Douglas is also diversified into large-scale computer services, including hospital systems.

The second prudent operating policy required 100 percent control over all profit centers. What would be more normal and sensible than, say, Johns-Manville or some other conventional corporation owning 100 percent of its profit centers, whether they were departments, groups, divisions, or subsidiaries? It would be neat and orderly, permit the company to have unchallengeable authority, funnel all the profits into the company, maximize flexibility in handling the unit, simplify accounting, obviate confusion in its management, personnel, and other policies, and so on. Besides, 100 percent control was the sound way to do business, as everyone knew.

With this prudent operating policy, a conventional corporation would start or acquire a new business, product line, or service on its own, without either the help or the hindrance of any outside partner. No customer, supplier, wholesaler, retailer, transportation service, source of financing, owner of related technology or R&D services—no one—would be permitted an equity, regardless of what he might contribute. True, there was an increasing number of exceptions, especially among the major petroleum and chemicals companies, but they remained exceptions.

Even today, all this sounds so sensible, so prudent. How could such a policy hamper the growth of conventional corporations?

In internal development, some of the disadvantages and lost growth opportunities due to 100 percent ownership have to do with the extreme difficulty of going it alone in all new product development efforts and the accelerated loss of extraordinarily fine talent.

In new products the failure rate was, and is, so high as to be beyond belief. We rarely see hard evidence, but it is generally accepted that some eight out of every ten new products fail. That means about 80 percent of all the new products fail after they have survived the hazards of conception, R&D, engineering, sometimes test marketing or pilot plants, and then production, distribution, and strong marketing introduction.

To make these costs and missed growth opportunities even more onerous, the life of products is shortening. Again, little hard evidence, but it is accepted that product life has probably been cut at least in half in the postwar generation, and may now be an average of only five years. Relative to the four to one odds against pulling off a successful new product, which might last only five years in the marketplace, the conventional manager can use all the help he can get. The conventional corporation has already used most of the experts it can hire or retain within its traditional policies, and still needs more help. Such help can include a range of outside creative, inventive, and other services.

Although there have been few other prudent solutions for the conventional corporations, we know that other alternatives exist. There are joint ventures and other "imprudent" forms of ownership to evoke the results that have been lacking. Even as superior a company as General Electric finally gave up its 100-percent-owned computer hardware business in favor of a jointly owned Honeywell-GE business. The combined business is now profitable, whereas GE had lost perhaps $100 million while going it alone. Observe, however, that this change in ownership involved a company, GE, that was much more flexible and aggressive than most large conventional companies, and that it came about only late in the postwar period, when some of management's conventions were crumbling.

The failures of operations with 100 percent ownership and the successes of some businesses with less than 100 percent ownership demonstrate that the prudent policy of total ownership and control was not, after all, always the best growth policy.

A second practical problem of the prudent operating policy of 100 percent ownership was the loss or unavailability of the rare individuals who could build businesses. This effect is harder to document than the preceding one, but it is just as real. Those few individuals who can make an order-of-magnitude difference in a business know they are worth far more than what is offered in regular executive compensation packages. They want, and can get, a piece of the action—and a hefty piece, not just a nominal piece. For example, in large conventional corporations, a rule of thumb usually restricts stock options to 5 percent of the total outstanding stock. Five percent for everyone, and "everyone" in large corporations may be 50 to 200 stock optionees, or more. Thus, the typical executive may eventually own some small fraction of one percent of the stock of a large corporation (whose stock price may be dormant anyway), whereas the entrepreneur almost never ends up with as little as 5 to 10 percent of his own medium-size business. One financing agreement of a start-up company in educational technology yielded a potential of 60 percent of the entire business to the founding group of five men. It becomes apparent that the kind of men who are most capable of producing growth are often those most repelled by the large restrictions and small compensation of the conventional corporation.

Similarly, the prudent operating policy of 100 percent ownership may restrict opportunities for acquisitions and mergers. For instance, less than 100 percent of a selling company may be available for purchase because of the complexities of estate holdings. Other stumbling blocks include the desire of the management of the selling company to retain some equity interest; the preference of private investors, or institutions, to hold some of the seller's stock longer; a difference of opinion on the sale of the business among several ownership groups; and the usual loss of a tax-loss carryforward if the acquirer holds more than 80 percent of the seller's stock after the acquisition.

However, the prudent operating policy calling for 100 percent control was overwhelmingly used by conventional corporations of the postwar generation. This meant, for example, that an otherwise desirable acquisition would be abandoned out of hand if the conventional acquirer could get his hands on, say, only 85 percent of the total amount of stock or assets.

Actually, the policy of requiring 100 percent ownership of each acquisition or merger has had several other depressant effects on growth; among them, some distortion of acquisition prices, protracted acquisition programs and efforts, and possible reductions in acquisition quality.

A case in point: After months of intensive acquisition searching, one acquirer listed on the New York Stock Exchange had the opportunity of looking at every potentially suitable drug and toiletry company.

He bought three of them, one at a price as low as seven times after-tax earnings, and got a rapidly growing company. All but one of the other dozens of situations were acquired by others within the ensuing several years, mostly at price-earnings multiples up to 20 or more. Many factors certainly pumped up the sellers' expectations, but one was the decreasing number of 100-percent-available sellers in the closed population of the then existing drug and toiletry companies.

Thus, the conventional corporations' prudent operating policies often yielded more prudence than growth. The policy of limited and narrow diversification often imprisoned companies within their own unattractive fields. The prudent operating policy of 100 percent ownership of all profit centers impeded new product and services development and reduced the attractiveness of conventional companies to those few people who have the unique ability to make businesses grow. It also led to acquisitions that were too expensive, too long delayed, or of less than specified quality.

PRUDENT FINANCIAL POLICY

On the other hand, how could a prudent *financial* policy possibly incur anything like the disadvantages of these prudent operating policies? A few lines of history will help explain.

Prudent financial policies were set forth in the 1950s, and even in the 1960s, by men whose experience and concepts had been forged in the 1930s and 1940s. Most of them—directors, investment bankers, commercial bankers, financial vice presidents, treasurers, and major stockholders—still had strong personal memories of the 1929 crash.

Two of the most common of the prudent financial policies should not have hurt anyone's reasonable growth: one was limiting the ratio of corporate debt to stockholders' equity; the other was insistence on a simple and clean financial structure for the corporation.

Almost everyone took it that a prudent debt ratio was an essential to corporate soundness. And so it was, and always will be. The difficulty is in combining that policy with consistent growth in earnings per share.

A frequent version of this prudent financial policy called for limiting the company's long-term debt to well under 50 percent of total capital. Granted that one usually did not get into trouble so long as he followed this policy, he would nevertheless come up against several well-recognized inhibitors to growth: limited leverage, difficult timing problems, and costly capital.

Limited leverage is the most familiar of this trio. Leverage is the use of borrowed capital instead of capital supplied by stockholders. The double-edged effect of leverage is to increase profits more than proportionally as the business grows and to decrease profits more than proportionally as the business declines. A corporation chooses between long-term debt and the selling of additional shares of its stock as a means of raising more capital for planned growth. The increase in earnings per share coming from new earnings could be twice as great in some cases if the corporation borrows—that is, uses leverage—than if it issues more stock. (The increase-in-earnings ratio, in practice, can be less, or even more, than two to one.)

In a soundly growing business, whenever the strong effects of leverage on earnings per share are limited to the standard and prudent ratio of debt to equity, growth is automatically corseted. However, to make the point unclear, it is a matter of degree: too little leverage, too little growth; too much leverage, excessively depressed earnings (or even disaster) at the next decline in earnings.

The second disadvantage of the prudent debt policy was that of timing problems. When limited by policy to a given proportion of long-term debt, a corporation must turn to the equity market for capital beyond the debt limit. However, borrowing is relatively easy compared with equity financing, especially public offerings of stock.

To oversimplify a fairly complex set of trade-offs in financial planning, it can take two or three times as long to complete a public offering of stock than a private placement of debt. The extra time required augments the company's risks of hitting an unfavorable market or of having to withdraw an equity offering altogether. Accordingly, an unnecessary dependence on equity financing caused by overprudent debt policy was a burden on some conventional corporations.

The third growth-inhibiting effect of prudent debt policy was the increased cost of capital. Fundamentally, the interest cost to the corporation on its debt is often materially lower than the cost of dividends paid on stock. Actually, in all these condensed examples of financial policy, the greatest cost to the conventional corporation may not have been merely the high cost of capital. There probably were instances when no financing was sought at all: when the prudent debt limit was reached and when the alternative of equity financing was too costly.

The second prudent financial policy that also had the unintended effect of impeding growth was that requiring the conventional corporation to have the simplest possible financial structure. A critic would state the same policy as requiring the minimum financial structure, not the optimum financial structure.

What, in context, was minimum? For most conventional industrial corporations, the simplest and desired financial structure traditionally consisted of one or two elements: one class of common stock and some long-term debt. No extra classes of common stock and no preferred stock, either convertible or straight. No warrants and no puts or calls issued by the corporation. Not too many different kinds of debts and no overdoing the convertibles. Usually no "units," or combination packages of two (or more) different kinds of securities, such as debentures with stock or common stock with warrants. Just the one- or two-part structure.

Prudent? Indeed it was. With the debt ratio already well—if not too well—in check, the restriction to common stock plus a simple debt structure could never itself put a conventional corporation into financial hot water through overextension. Too, the security analysts, institutional investors, and the small odd-lot investors could all easily understand the structure. The policy also sensibly avoided the risk of a conventional corporation appearing either unsound in its financial management or unduly promotional. The simple capital structure minimized future dilution of stockholders' equity, tended to be least costly in terms of fixed interest and fixed dividend requirements, and was simple and inexpensive to administer.

The disadvantages, infrequently voiced by conventional corporations, were at least equally material. Primarily, the prudent financial policy of a simple capital structure sometimes restricted the total capital that a corporation might sensibly raise. Secondarily, it complicated the maintenance of corporate control, increased the risks of depending on the always uncertain capital markets, and estranged the conventional corporation from some sources of capital.

The restriction on sound capital additions occurred in terms of both capital for acquisitions and mergers and capital for other reasonable corporate uses. Let us take acquisitions for stock first. In this case, a corporation literally creates new capital by issuing shares of its stock to pay the sellers for their company. For example, when Norton Simon, Inc., completed its acquisition of Max Factor & Co. in 1973, it issued its common stock, valued at over $400 million. That created a lot of new capital—more than is created by most of the individual public offerings of corporate stock.

If one rejects the alternative of dropping good acquisition prospects because of problems involving the acquirer's common stock, what are the remaining alternatives? Well, just about none, in terms of the prudent financial policy of one class of common stock and some long-term debt. One of the uncounted acquisitions lost just this way involved a company that had plummeted from being a high flyer on the American Stock Exchange to a price below its book value, a price decline of more than 90 percent. The company, seeking acquisitions as a part of its turnaround, stuck to offering its common stock to sellers, who lacked the temperament and resources to be interested in this speculative stock. Unwilling to use other forms of capital, the acquirer failed to attract a particular desired seller, who was simultaneously being courted by other would-be acquirers. These competitors did have a range of stock plans, cash plans, and debt plans, and one of them eventually consummated the acquisition. In fact, all the competing acquirers were able to make other acquisitions, while the acquirer who was restricted to his common stock made none.

To generalize from this and a host of other capital-short situations: One reason for capital malnutrition and the resulting thwarted growth is the policy that makes a corporation root for its capital in a narrow or empty trough. The problem in these cases is not a lack of sufficient size or worth in the acquirer, but a policy restriction on the nature of its financial structure that, to some, is artificial.

A conventional corporation can put itself into a comparable box regarding the creation of capital for corporate needs other than acquisitions. In this case, the capital is created through the financial markets rather than through the issue of some form of capital to the sellers of a company. By prudent policy, the corporation has authorized, or will authorize, only a straight debt issue, such as bonds or notes. The market may insist on a convertible debt, or notes with warrants, or some other variant of debt-financing arrangements. The corporation cannot satisfy the market and does not get its capital.

The several secondary faults of the simplest capital structure policy can also be costly. The control problem mentioned above is another that is rarely voiced in public, and the public rarely thinks of it. In the chief executive's office and in the boardroom it comes up often, with no beating around the bush. Look at a publicly held company that has never had any publicized control problems: no takeover attempts, no proxy fights. Still, the control is held by a board, a management group, and dependable friends who own maybe 20 percent of the common shares outstanding. Top management, after nearly two years of searching and disappointments, finds a good, compatible company that wants to merge, at a tolerable price. But it is discovered that the number of shares needed to buy the company comes too close to the number of shares that now control the would-be acquirer. The deal is off, because the acquirer is prevented by policy from issuing preferred stock or other equity shares that would have both satisfied the seller and protected the buyer's control of the combined business.

To recap: The prudent financial policy that limited debt financing to low levels until the late 1960s incurred the disadvantages of decreased growth in earnings per share in a period of economic growth, difficulties and delays in getting financing, and higher costs for the capital obtained. The prudent financial policy of preserving the simplest corporate financial structure had advantages, but the growth of conventional corporations was often impeded by the overriding disadvantages, which involved serious restrictions on the creation of needed corporate capital, aggravation of problems of keeping control of the corporation, increased risks of depending on the uncertain capital markets, and the estrangement of the company from some sources of capital.

Now does it seem strange that large conventional corporations as a group had average earnings-per-share growth from 1967 to 1972 of only 3.6 percent per year—including inflation? The prudent policies cited were only a few of the many practiced by these companies. It should now be clear that these policies, hammered out of experience going back to the 1929 crash and the 1937 recession, did not combine a growth thrust with their innate soundness.

THE RULES OF THE GAME

Sprinkle into this situation a third set of factors—what I call the consensual constraints on certain management activities that could otherwise contribute to growth. The consensual constraints, or "rules of the game," barred things that, as the English say, "aren't done"—not by executive gentlemen in polite corporate society, that is.

Three typical rules of the game that were generally binding on conventional corporations in the postwar generation were very limited divestments of unsuccessful or unwanted businesses, no raids on other companies, and no private antitrust suits against other companies. These rules are very different from one another. All three, however, represent still other self-imposed restraints that also adversely affected the growth of conventional corporations.

In our day of accelerating spin-offs, split-offs, divestments, and other maneuvers, it is already difficult to remember or even believe that corporate managements in most of the postwar period rarely sold off a profitless or ill-fitting business. There were exceptions: General Foods sold off its shrimp and condiment businesses in 1952 and Bristol-Myers divested its Sun Tube and Rubberset divisions in 1956. Such notable exceptions came about because, to some, this unspoken rule made little sense.

Even the best managements made and inherited mistakes, but they would have done better to face them early and get out of those businesses that could not or should not be made profitable and useful to the main body of the corporation. Such rarely acknowledged concepts as corporation pride, embarrassment, tradition, and stubbornness perhaps best account for the widespread hanging on to losers.

The ultimately successful experience of a builder of complex industrial machinery points up the general unwisdom of shunning divestments. The machinery builder, whose business was profitable and growing, had acquired a company that manufactured electric motors, expecting to obtain both a captive source of motors for its own machinery and another profitable business. The plan did not work on either count. Just before the final decision to close it down, management decided at least to take a look at the alternative of selling the division, which had lost more than a million dollars. Eventually, the machinery builder, instead of liquidating, sold for over $100,000 more than the liquidating value.

A second rule of the game for many conventional corporations in the postwar world was never to raid, never to seek to take control of another company if its management were unwilling. My questioning of this rule should provoke sharp disagreement in the business community, so deeply held is the feeling against all forms of forced takeovers. Some adventurers might stoop so low. Louis Wolfson, later jailed for securities violations, did try unsuccessfully to take over American Motors from George Romney.

There is, however, another side to the story, which has almost never seen the light of day. At any given time, some publicly held companies are declining or failing. Some of these could be rescued and rebuilt, to the advantage of most employees, the communities involved, the stockholders, and the suppliers. What happens? Sometimes the entrenched management cannot seem to rebuild but will not yield control. Often, the management represents only itself, holding only a small percentage of the stock of its failing company. Some people would advise filing a stockholder derivative suit, a long and tenuous process. Others would prefer simply to let time take its course. Still others say that a take-over of such a sick corporation would benefit not only the attacking group, but everyone involved, except for the management group that permitted the decline of the business.

At this point, the conventional corporation does not come in. It passes up valuable assets at a rare bargain price and fails to take control, rebuild, and restore the values still alive in the sick company.

The umbrage that will be taken at questioning this rule of the game will probably be out of proportion to its importance to the growth problems of conventional corporations. Narrowly, this rule against forced take-overs has probably limited the growth of only a few conventional corporations in the past 25 years. Broadly, however, this gentlemanly rule calls attention to conventional corporations' constrained resourcefulness, aggressiveness, and flexibility, just as the rule against divestitures did.

Let us look at just one more rule of the game, to show another facet of the underlying constraints on the growth of conventional corporations. This rule was never, never to sue another company for antitrust violations against you. There was merit to this rule, as there was to the others. The threat of antitrust litigation, when unjustified, can be a terrible depressant on the unjustly accused corporation. The high cost of executive and legal time is the least cost. The greatest costs are the excessive caution, the passing up of legitimate opportunities, and the multiplication of legalistic interference in normal business activities.

Still, one could argue that the failure to prosecute clear and damaging antitrust invasions is as wrong as falsely claiming violations when none exist. The antitrust story is not over. In fact it has just begun. A later chapter of Part One looks at antitrust actions in relation to the coming of the supercorporation. At that point, the recent rapid growth of antitrust suits by one corporation against another is further discussed. This movement is thoroughly breaking the old rule that pervaded management attitudes since World War II.

In summary, then, certain unspoken rules of the corporate game have prevented conventional corporations from achieving their growth potential. One rule bound most conventional corporations to swallow the majority of their unsuccessful and unwanted businesses, rather than to admit their mistakes openly by divesting the units. This rule, which cost both money and jobs, has since been retired by general consent, and there is now a sizable and growing volume of divestitures and spin-offs.

A second rule prohibited forcible take-overs of other corporations, thus contributing somewhat to the growth problems of conventional corporations. More important, it further stifled their aggressiveness, flexibility, and imagination.

The rule of the game that discouraged the legal defense of the conventional corporation against serious antitrust violations has probably hurt corporate growth in a few instances. This rule is another representation of the broader limitations on aggressiveness and flexibility that are major inhibitors of corporate growth.

From a bang-up start to the whimper of waning growth—this was the story of many conventional corporations in the postwar generation. The growth rates of large corporations as a group, cited above, slowed to a typical increase in earnings per share of under 5 percent per year for five years at the end of the generation.

Were there no other ways? Hardly so. Three different kinds of companies were outperforming the conventional corporations: the handful of growth companies, such as Polaroid; the incredibly successful foreign companies in the United States market such as Sony and Volkswagen; and, apparently, the swinging conglomerates of the 1960s. The large growth companies are so few in number, their success so rare, that one could not sensibly expect most or all of a thousand or so other large U.S. corporations to change into growth companies like IBM or Xerox. Similarly, the great productivity and other natural advantages of the leading foreign companies in U.S. domestic markets would not provide a practical model.

The conglomerates of the 1960s were something else. One of the basic ideas in this book is that the unusual behavior of the conglomerates has already had a vast effect on an increasing number of conventional corporations—an effect mostly unnoticed by the public, economists, or the government. This is the third of the historical forces opening up the future for supercorporations.

What the conglomerates did, and the evidences of their mental transplants into conventional corporate minds, are documented in the next chapter.

3

THE SWINGING CONGLOMERATES
of the 1960s

No CONVENTIONAL ADJECTIVE, such as "aggressive," "imaginative," or "fast-growing," conveys the frenzy and the long run of luck that characterized the conglomerates of the 1960s. They were truly "swinging," and for a time it seemed that they would never stop swinging. Now even widows and orphans know that the conglomerates' ups and downs were wild. But in order to understand the insinuating influence of the swinging conglomerates on the minds of the managers of conventional corporations, a closer look at those conglomerates is basic.

The Ups

Litton Industries, contrary to popular belief, did not start it all. Litton for a time was the most prominent, but its rise was preceded by a series of crashing failures that were merchandised far less cleverly than the more familiar 1960 conglomerates.

Many of today's middle managers, bankers, security analysts, and investors scarcely remember the names of U.S. Hoffman, Penn-Dixie Industries, Merritt, Chapman & Scott, and Aeronca, Inc. Each started small, made a quick series of acquisitions, snared wide publicity, had colorful headmen, were among the top performers in the stock market—and then declined or collapsed. Almost any executive could tell you exactly why these so-called wheeler-dealers failed. They did not buy good companies in some cases, added nothing, often milked their acquisitions, and simply built a house of cards with the help of slick accounting methods. Of course they failed. With these demonstrations of the folly of attempting corporate perpetual motion, the business and financial community could settle back to observing the conventional corporations, the too rare growth companies, and the first hints of serious foreign competitors right here at home.

Then, along came Litton.

Litton started in 1953 by purchasing three privately held companies with combined sales of about $3 million. This began a chain of reported quarter-to-quarter increases in earnings per share that lasted for 57 straight quarters. From the original $3 million, sales grew to over $1.8 billion in 1968, when the earnings record collapsed, to the tune of a Litton statement that management problems had caused the debacle. In that year, Litton's profits were reported to be $116 million.

Encouraged by Litton's record, a booming economy, plastic accounting arrangements, and a loving stock market, dozens of new, Litton-type entrepreneurs started their own conglomerates.

The up, or the rocketlike growth, of the conglomerates depended squarely on flagrant violations of the prudent policies of the conventional corporations and on some special tricks of the trade, too.

To begin with, the conglomerates gained their very identity by flying in the face of prudent operating policy No. 1: they recognized few limits on their diversification. Bangor Punta Corp., starting with the drying bones of a small railroad and the shell of a Cuban sugar business nationalized by Fidel Castro, put itself into dress and drapery fabrics, pleasure boats, engineering services, sewage treatment plants, and emblematic jewelry, to name only some of its commitments.

Questor Corp. managed to get into an eerie spread that brought together distilled beverages, publishing, china and tableware, cigars, home furnishings, jewelry, electric housewares, toys, baby pants, and a chain of auto diagnostic centers in Spain. Not bad for a previously solid Toledo, Ohio, company that for 30 years had produced auto exhaust systems for the aftermarket. In fact, this was singularly adventurous for a company that started its acquiring within its own industry by taking on a maker of inefficient shock absorbers. The deal was so bad that the Questor president said, "I should have been canned."

The shattering swing from the conventionals' too-restricted diversification to the conglomerates' crazy-quilt collections can also be seen in Rapid-American Corporation. It, and a predecessor, Glen Alden, were in and out of a dozen companies in coal, fire engines, printing and electroplating, and others before Rapid-American settled down to a more conventional mix of liquor, retail chains, clothing, and luggage.

Second, the conglomerates, while preferring to buy 100 percent of their acquisitions, as in prudent operating policy No. 2, were more likely to settle for less. It did not hurt earnings-per-share growth, and nothing dare delay the pace of deal closings. City Investing Co. in 1971 owned 49 percent of General Development Corp. and 53 percent of Guerdon Industries, for example.

Third, the prudent financial policy of a conservative debt ratio—do we need to finish the sentence? The conglomerates were able to find lenders of massive amounts of money. Ling-Temco-Vought by the end of 1971 had corporate debt of over a half billion dollars, as against net losses in 1969, 1970, and 1971 totaling $165 million. Boise Cascade not only got itself into land development, leisure homes, and mobile homes, but it also acquired the magazine *Psychology Today,* an engineering consulting firm, recreational vehicles, and others. Along the way, Boise Cascade was able to accumulate a total of $507 million of long-term debt by 1971. Its 1971 gross revenues were $1.8 billion and its net loss was $85 million. By 1973 Boise Cascade's investment bankers announced that they had been able to arrange "the restructuring of long-term indebtedness of $346 million." This restructuring was needed after Boise Cascade had sold off hundreds of millions of dollars' worth of its properties as a means of survival.

Fourth, the conglomerates obviously could not exist with the prudent financial policy of keeping the simplest capital structure. In an extreme case, ITT was listed in standard financial manuals as having 15 different issues of long-term debt and an additional 17 different issues of capital stock.

Fifth, some of the conglomerates were willing to break the conventional rule of the game and do a little corporate raiding. Litton used a touch of this kind of persuasion on Hewitt-Robins Inc., which then quickly decided to join up. Glen Alden Co., itself now absorbed by Rapid-American Corp., made a pass at the largest wholesale drug company, McKesson & Robbins, Inc., but in this instance the attempted raid was a failure.

Sixth, there were a few early divestments during the heyday, breaking another rule of the conventional game.

So much for the conglomerates' 1.000 batting average in breaking the policies and rules by which most conventional corporations lived, or at least existed. Still more artistry was required for the full conglomerate effect. The most inspired efforts involved the pooling of interest, certain other special accounting treatments, plus public relations blitzes that had to be seen to be believed.

The phrase "pooling of interest" was gibberish to most investors, but meant the stuff of growth to the conglomerateur. The pooling of interest accomplished two miracles at one blow. It gave—literally gave—large chunks of instant earnings to the conglomerate by the stroke of the pen and at once protected those earnings against the otherwise frequent accounting requirement of specified write-downs.

To put it in plain arithmetic and English, say that a conglomerate is likely to earn $10 million in a given business year that ends December 31. Say that this conglomerate buys a company earning $2 million, closing the transaction in late December. The seller's earnings would do the conglomerate almost no good in the last few days of December. Wrong. Just qualify the deal as a pooling of interest and, abracadabra, the conglomerate earned the full $2 million for that year, which the seller also earned. In this example, the conglomerate just penciled in a 20 percent profit increase by getting that deal onto its books before the end of December.

The magic is even more wonderful. The purchase price often was far above the seller's own book valuation of his business, as carried on his balance sheet. This margin of the acquisition price over the net book value, called goodwill, normally had to be written off against profits. But the same magic, pooling of interest, also wiped out the threatened write-down of profits. This was too flagrant to last, and poolings have since been severely restricted by accounting authorities.

The second accounting vehicle involved other special treatments that also increased earnings by the stroke of the pen. There were many of these, but one of the more clever will stand for the whole pack. In the early days of the conglomerates, before they and other forces helped to bid acquisition prices to all-time highs, Gulf + Western Industries began picking up a number of small distributors of auto parts for the aftermarket, buying many of them below their book value. There was, in just one year, a total of hundreds of thousands of dollars of excess of the sellers' aggregate book values over G + W's total purchase prices. Put it on G + W's balance sheet? No—it is really operating profit, just like the profit you earn from running a business, so just add those excess book value figures to regular profits. This little special provided about 25 percent of all of G + W's operating profit in one growth year.

Another essential for the conglomerates' ups was, of course, public relations. A complex of millions of potential participants had to be transformed into being true believers, or at least compliant performers. These included owners of potential acquisitions for the conglomerates, news media, and the conglomerates' own people—plus the corps of state and federal regulators, public accountants, attorneys, bankers, security analysts, credit services, and all of the others needed to support the conglomerate movement.

To be just, it must be emphasized that the conglomerates were not alone in putting together a fanciful world of unending growth, easy stock market winnings, and all the rest. The entire era was all of a piece, as wonderfully described by John Brooks,[1] "Adam Smith," [2] and others. You did not have to be taken in by the conglomerate promoters. You could just as well have lost in the overpromising, overpromoted hedge funds, "story" stocks, funds specializing in investment letter stocks, and the whole array of stock market games that so many played and lost. Our interest, however, is in the special part the conglomerates and their nifty public relations played in fixing the conglomerate ideas and methods more firmly in the business mind than their fanciest artists could have imagined.

The conglomerates' artistry in public relations wooed us with what we greedily wanted to hear—that extremely rapid growth could be manufactured by many more companies than IBM, Xerox, and a handful of accepted growth companies. This artistry was some of the most

[1] *The Go-Go Years* (New York: Weybright & Talley, 1973).
[2] *The Money Game* (New York: Random House, 1968); *Supermoney* (New York: Random House, 1972).

persuasive corporate public relations ever invented; its excellence far surpassed conglomerate managements' attempts to operate the businesses they were picking up so quickly.

It is now almost as hard to portray the go-go appeal that enveloped the conglomerates and their adoring public as it would be to give you the full flavor of the Flapper Era of an earlier decade. But this replay will give you a little of the swinging essence of the 1960 conglomerate story.

New catchwords were helpful to the ploy, so we were given dandy little companies that had just become "synergistic," "congeneric," "multimarket," or even "free form." At the start of the adventure most of the companies had only limited assets, but the assets of acquired and merged companies were definitely to be "pluralized," "rationalized," or "redeployed." These fabrications helped us to accept the claims that almost any quickly accumulating bunch of unrelated companies would surely support annual profits growth of 15 to 30 percent per year, compounded, for many years to come.

Few publishers today could afford to reprint the luscious multicolored annual and other reports, which were marvelously designed and printed on the finest paper stock. In these, names could be important, too. The old and solid A P Parts Corp. became Questor, the name selected because it projected an image of zest and progress. Said Questor in a typical promotional piece of the era, "This is the Age of Change. Questor was conceived to lead. Questor's age—the Age of Aquarius."

The only thing more fatuous than this sort of conglomerate public relations was the audience reactions. One security analyst's recommendation to buy Questor is inane enough to speak for the era of the swinging conglomerates. Questor was ". . . a whole lot of bright guys doing important things together." Audience reactions helped move the stock of Questor up from 17¼ to 35½ within 1968; but by 1971 it was back down around 18.

Questor, noted above for its slapstick diversification, ended 1970 with a net loss in its acquired nonautomotive businesses, but its public relations had helped for a time to turn the merry-go-round. Earnings, after extraordinary items, rose from $10.7 million in 1965 to a peak of $19.7 million in 1969, followed by a drop to $5.9 million in 1970, Questor's worst year. After a few more seesaw years, Questor earned $11.1 million in 1973—some $400,000 more than nine years before in

1965. That profit increase, under 4 percent in a total of nine years, somehow tells you more about Questor, swinging conglomerates, and their public relations than the public relations blitz itself ever told you. One more audience reaction: the Questor stock that fell to 18 in 1971 was, by mid-1974, idling in the price range of 12⅜ to 7.

The foregoing seven tactics—from strange diversification to manic public relations—had a lot to do with the unheard-of ''growth'' of the 1960 conglomerates. The excessive use of these and similar tactics also had a lot to do with the crashes of most of the conglomerates toward the end of that decade.

Still, the memory lingers on, and it will be seen later that the conventional corporations are getting their feet wetter and wetter in some of the waters in which the conglomerates once disported all by themselves.

The Downs

The downs of the conglomerates are also instructive for would-be copiers of their tactics and methods.

The falling out of bed was famous, but at this distance in time, it may be useful to recall a few of the record downs of the conglomerates. The stocks of a group of six of them dropped in price by an average of more than 90 percent, as shown in Table 1. This list of

Table 1. **Drops in stock prices of some conglomerates.**

Conglomerate Company	1962–72 High	Year Set	1962–73 * Low	Year Set	Percent Decrease
A-T-O Inc. (formerly Automatic Sprinkler)	74	1968	6	1970	92
Boise Cascade	80¼	1969	8¼	1973	90
LTV (formerly Ling-Temco-Vought)	169½	1967	7⅝	1971	95
Litton	120⅜	1967	8½	1973	93
Republic	92	1968	2¼	1973	98
Whittaker	94⅜	1967	5¼	1973	95

* To April 1973.

companies is not intended to be representative of the more solid conglomerates. We are simply recalling the dizzying enthusiasm for almost any company that promised greater growth than did the conventional corporations—and the downs that came when the promises proved hollow.

For many of the downed flyers, their stock market downs persisted. By mid-1974 only Boise Cascade was selling substantially above its all-time low. Still, at its "recovery" price of 17, Boise Cascade was selling for just 21 percent of its 1969 high price of 80¼. The much longer casualty list includes similarly persistent downs for Alco Standard (from an all-time high stock price of 40½ to a mid-1974 price of 8), Arcata National (53⅛ to 8), Monogram (81¾ to 5), Rapid-American (52½ to 13), and so on. By mid-1974 some of the downed conglomerates had shucked off some of their worst losers and had otherwise tightened up operations. Ironically, most of their stock prices remained down, partly because of continued disenchantment with conglomerates and partly because of a bear market generally.

The shattering downs of the once-swinging conglomerates can be pictured in ways other than their 75 to 95 percent declines in stock prices. Take the unpublicized case example of Hathaway Instruments, Inc., which started out in 1959 as rapidly as had National General, Commonwealth United, or other more familiar performers. The fashionable conglomerateur James J. Ling, who was very impressive to the financial world as the head of LTV Inc., took an interest in the Hathaway Instruments Division of the old Hamilton Watch Company. At its 1959 starting point, this little sideline of Mr. Ling's had sales of $4.7 million and profits of $371,000. In 1960 it made five acquisitions and suddenly had sales of $15.9 million and profits of $805,000.

Along the way, a conventional manufacturer of electrical controls, which was well financed and long on assets but short on growth, almost succumbed to the razzle-dazzle wooing of Hathaway Industries. Then a hard-nosed financial consultant spoiled the affair by telling the intended bride some of Hathaway's shortcomings as a marriage partner. Later, Hathaway itself merged into another of the publicized promotions of the period, Lionel Corp. Still later, in Lionel's own collapse, a division of Hathaway was spun out, with the expectable downs. Its sales in 1973 were $6.6 million with a $131,000 deficit. This deficit followed a profit of $64,000 in 1972 and a loss of $157,000 in 1971—down from the 1959 profits, which we saw were $371,000.

The downs of the conglomerates can be understood further—and hopefully avoided by today's more aggressive conventional corporations—through a thorough understanding of how the conglomerates could fall so fast from record growth to staggering losses. A brief case example provides a red flag for a typical failing, buying too fast.

Consider the acquisition technique of Gulf + Western, as I observed it one day in the Southeast. I was meeting that day with the owner of an engine rebuilding company, beginning to explore the mutual advantages of his selling to another company interested in the auto aftermarket. Then, in some embarrassment, the owner asked me to leave him at about 11:00 A.M. and come back after lunch. It seems that he had been backed into seeing two different buyers that day, and the appointments overlapped. As I left the interrupted meeting, the flustered owner introduced me to the Gulf + Western representative, who was about to have his first meeting with the seller.

Returning after lunch, I suppose I should not have been surprised to hear from the owner that Gulf + Western had already made an offer to buy his business for a specified price per share and specified terms, subject of course to G + W study and audit of the seller. You see, it took Gulf + Western in this case almost three hours to put together its buy offer.

For our final illustration, we are indebted to the 1973 prospectus used by Litton Industries in selling one of its 1967 acquisitions to the public. In October of that year Litton acquired Stouffer, the frozen food and restaurant company, for $100 million of Litton stock. The pounding public relations campaign said that the sophisticated conglomerate would help its acquired companies to grow further. Fact: Stouffer, under Litton's wing, acquired the Hanscom Bros. Bakery, which lost $700,000, after tax benefits, in its three full years in Litton/Stouffer. Of course, the conglomerate would also help its acquired partners with financing. Fact: Litton financial advances cost Stouffer 8 percent per year, whereas long-term Stouffer borrowing from other sources cost from 6 percent to 6.88 percent.

Then we have the so-called advantage of the conglomerate's management team helping the acquired companies, thereby rendering those needful acquired managements far better off than they had been before they sold out to their betters. Fact: Litton, like most other companies, charges its operating units a management fee. Litton, and conglomerates generally, are not the only parent groups whose management fees are decried by the operating managements who are forced to pay them.

Nevertheless, Litton's own prospectus helps give the lie to its claims to be adding something to its component companies. Actually, there was a subtraction amounting to millions of dollars. In 1968, Litton charged Stouffer $997,000 in management fees, but Stouffer management reported in the Litton prospectus that it could have gotten those same services for $308,000. In 1969, the excess Litton fee was $797,000; 1970, $886,000; 1971, $810,000; 1972, $887,000; 1973, nearly $500,000. The total excess charges Litton levied on Stouffer in five and a half years was approximately $4.5 million.

Finally, the superior growth of conglomerates was represented to come significantly from the internal growth of acquired companies—certainly not from inflating earnings reports by tricky financial and accounting practices. This genuine growth must have occurred in some of the thousands of companies acquired by the conglomerates.

Fact: In the Litton/Stouffer deal, with Stouffer having grown well before joining Litton, Stouffer profits went down from $2.6 million in 1968 (the first full year in Litton) to $2.2 million in 1971. Profits, excluding a nonrecurring gain, were up in 1972 to $2.8 million. By 1973, Stouffer was to be sold. So Stouffer's total conglomerate-style profit growth was $200,000, or less than 10 percent, in four years and not enough to offset inflation.

To summarize this one peek inside the archtypical conglomerate: Litton failed to produce growth in Stouffer while charging Stouffer heavily for being in Litton. With this sorry experience repeated in Litton and most other conglomerates, they had to crash, and they did.

The Persistence of Conglomerate Ideas

All this, and bales more, would be easier to write, and to read, as fiction—though it is all fact, much of it duly reported in accordance with generally accepted accounting principles. Unlike the way cheap fiction might tell it, the swinging conglomerates of the 1960s were not swept from the scene with the conglomerate crash of May 1970, when nearly all their stocks nose-dived. Rather, in new forms and adaptations just being evolved by conventional corporations, a version of the conglomerate idea is entering upon a far greater life than it had known with the 30 or so swingers in the previous decade.

It is so surprising as to be unbelievable that the conventional corporations have adopted so much of the conglomerates' tactics and methods as their own. To fertilize the crossbreeding, some conventional corporations have been hiring top executives from conglomerates, after the conglomerates' fall, to run conventional corporations. Harry J. Gray, formerly senior executive vice president and No. 3 man of Litton Industries, was brought in as president and chief administrative officer of United Aircraft Corp. The latter had 1972 sales of $2 billion and earnings of $50.6 million (in 1971, a deficit of $44 million) as compared to Litton's fiscal 1972 sales of $2.5 billion and deficit per share of $.14. Other prominent conglomerate executives can similarly be expected to be installed in conventional corporations.

Whether or not the fascination of the conventional corporations' managers and directors with the conglomerates can be explained logically, it is a fact of life. It is the third historical force opening the door of the future to supercorporations. The first force, you will recall, is the age-old urge to grow, supported by national and world economies that allow at least some dozens of large corporations to grow at double the average rates.

The second historical force is the failure of most conventional corporations to grow as rapidly as their urge—and the burgeoning economy—permits. This has led conventional managers to a disenchantment with their prudent operating and financial policies.

I predict that the three forces are combining to produce in the 1970s and 1980s from one to several dozen supercorporations plus scores of semisupers. The supers will usually have the body of a large conventional corporation and some of the heart and mind of the swinging conglomerate. But the new supercorporations, each starting with the resources of a billion-dollar base, are going to be stronger, sounder, less promotional, better managed, and less vulnerable to business catastrophe than the 1960 conglomerates. They should also command higher price-earnings multiples than either the large conventional corporations or today's deflated 1960 conglomerates.

Some natural objections have been voiced to the idea of supercorporations, and these must now be dealt with.

4

FIVE CHALLENGES to the SUPERCORPORATE CONCEPT

BEFORE DEVOTING the rest of this volume to analyzing the expected emergence of the postindustrial supercorporations and semisupers, we should give our attention to five basic challenges to the notion of supers. The first challenge has to do with the antitrust hazard to any super that may emerge; the other four question the validity of the very concept of supercorporations as realistic and as representing a truly new corporate form. The challenges are:

Antitrust interference. Won't antitrust stop the supercorporations before they are fairly started? If so, this is a good place to stop talking about supers.

Retrenching of conventional corporations. A lot of these companies are backing out of some of their looser diversification. Aren't they becoming "antisupers" or "nonsupers" and leading the whole corporate parade in the opposite direction?

Repurchasing of stock. The conventional corporations have spent billions of dollars to take tens of millions of shares of their stock off the market. Isn't this another form of retrenching, and what is so supercorporation-oriented about this trend?

Sufficiency of raw materials. Are there now enough billion-dollar corporations to supply the future stock of supers?

Multinationals versus supercorporations. Even if there are to be supers, aren't they already here, and doesn't everyone else call them multinationals?

The concept of supercorporations, as originated here, surmounts these five objections and looks a bit more real after being tested against them.

Antitrust Interference *

One of the toughest hazards of the supercorporation could be antitrust law and regulation. After all, large U.S. corporations that are less than supers are sometimes successfully prosecuted for anticompetitive activities. Also, such corporations are far more frequently deterred by the specter of prosecution.

If conventional corporations, large and small, and a few conglomerates have so many antitrust problems, why look at architects' drawings of a supercorporation, which should be easily aborted by antitrust?

After admitting that few can understand or predict antitrust matters, let us look at both the pros and the cons of antitrust versus the supercorporation. The odds greatly favor the supers surviving the antitrust war, while losing some bruising battles along the way.

Taking the negatives first, there are three: the usual U.S. antitrust attacks on large corporations; the increase in private antitrust suits, which I predict will multiply; and the brand-new European consciousness of antitrust. The first hazard is familiar, so let us look at the latter two.

Private antitrust suits need a little introduction. Since 1890, antitrust complaints have traditionally been brought by the federal government, not by corporations. Within the past five years, however, an increasing number of antitrust suits have been started by one corporation against another. For example, competitors, including Control Data Corp. and Itel, have filed antitrust suits against IBM. Control Data later negotiated a lush settlement with IBM, only one part of which involved Control Data's acquiring IBM's Service Bureau Corp. for its

* This section deals only with the antitrust activity that appears to be mainly antiacquisition in nature. Excluded are price-fixing cases, such as the blockbuster action against General Electric, Westinghouse, and other electrical equipment manufacturers in the late 1950s.

book value of $16 million. Trade sources valued the Service Bureau Corp. at a minimum of $30 million, and some said $50 million. Also, Eastman Kodak has been the target of large, private antitrust actions.

My prediction of the multiplying of private antitrust suits has begun to prove itself already. Of the recent spate of new legal actions, one is so astounding that I am including it here. In 1974 AT&T, a national monopoly, filed suit against MCI Communications Inc., charging that MCI had illegally attempted to monopolize the private-line communications market dominated by AT&T. MCI revenues from this market in 1973 were $200,000; AT&T's were $1 billion—5,000 times larger than MCI's. Strange as this case is, it does reaffirm the idea that private antitrust actions are on the rise.

Whether private antitrust suits are justified as benefiting competition, or whether they are a cynical means of adding up to tens of millions of dollars to the successful attacker's treasury, is difficult to establish. In either case, it is certain that private antitrust litigation will continue to increase. At the same time, government efforts will continue and increase, regardless of other considerations. Both government and private actions will add up to a marked increase in the antitrust hazards of large and successful corporations. A very rough prediction is that any of the more than 350 U.S. companies in the billion-dollar class (sales or assets) is an easy and likely target; a few in the half-billion-dollar class are also going to find themselves in court, each time with legal bills in the hundreds of thousands or millions of dollars, within the next five years.

As for European antitrust, had this book been written just a few years earlier, there would have been no basis for noting any. European antitrust? It was as prevalent as consumer advertising in Russia before 1950. Now, however, two large American companies have been prosecuted. In one case, the Commission of the European Communities in 1973 fined Pittsburgh Corning Europe S.A. the equivalent of $113,000. The charge was selling cellular glass insulating material for a higher price in Germany than in Belgium and Holland. The company stopped the practice, paid the fine, and did not appeal the case.

With the prospect of increasing antitrust hazards, who has the courage or the folly to try to become a supercorporation? Why even talk about it? Because there is a strong other side to the story. Throughout the history of antitrust, we somehow find great growth of some large corporations, by internal growth, acquisitions, or both. We also find tight and occasionally increasing concentrations of an industry's business in a few corporate hands.

After all, the 1970 U.S. Census shows again what has hardly been news: that 75 percent of the industrial gases are sold by the four largest companies in that industry; that sales of refrigerators and freezers are similarly concentrated (82 percent); that four manufacturers in each industry have cornered 91 percent of truck and bus sales and 92 percent of light bulb sales; and so on. Moreover, in the period from 1967 to 1970, the four largest companies in some other industries increased their proportion of shipments: pesticides (39 to 47 percent), canned and smoked seafood (44 to 53 percent), alkalis and chlorine (63 to 71 percent); and there were others.

Thus, antitrust enforcement in the United States works, and it does not. It protects competition by defeating monopoly and oligopoly, and it does not. Twenty books will not resolve this paradox, nor the confusion or ambivalence of businessmen, financiers, and the public about it. However, we have resolved the far smaller question of whether antitrust action will kill the forthcoming supercorporations while they are aborning.

Retrenching of Conventional Corporations

The $750 billion U.S. business community is big enough to accommodate a variety of different opinions, with each one supported by correct findings of fact.

To some observers, the conventional corporations have been pulling their horns in, starting in the 1969–1971 recession and continuing into the succeeding business boom and downturn. The conventional companies, by selling off or liquidating numbers of more or less unrelated loss centers, are, after all, getting back to their basic businesses. As this happens, these people say, the possibility of widely diversified, extra-aggressive supercorporations just doesn't wash. This is the opposite of our categorical prediction of the rise of a group of extremely diversified giant corporations. So we have some conflicting evidence to sift.

There are hundreds of examples of corporate pullbacks. The Travelers Corp., the big insurance company, got rid of five noninsurance businesses that some people did not even know Travelers had. It sold its television station in Hartford, Connecticut, two radio stations (one owned since 1924), much of the computer leasing business of Randolph Computer (acquired in 1969), and a small data processing service business.

More companies have been cutting back. Aluminum Company of America sold all its New York City apartment buildings, which were among its largest real estate holdings. International Paper Co. sold the Donald L. Bren Co., a Southern California home developer, to its original owner.

None of the transactions just mentioned was the result of a government order. All these divestments, and many more, are evidence of retrenching by conventional corporations.

At the other pole of this question, conventional corporations are not all cutting back; some are continuing to spread out into new and broader spheres of diversification. The contest between these two contrary trends is an important force that will affect whether or not the United States will have supercorporations.

I conclude that the net trend will be to greater diversification for conventional corporations, after allowing for considerable and continuing retrenchments by some of them, some of the time. Much of the evidence for this conclusion is presented later in Part One, when this and other forewarnings of the supers are considered.

At this point, the experience of one conventional corporation illustrates the diversification trend, which I believe to be dominant over the cutbacks. The company, Cerro Corp., has had a long-term history of cyclical results and often low profits. More recently, its Chilean copper mines were nationalized, while the status of those in Peru became shaky. Cerro embarked on diversification by acquisition. It purchased, among other companies, Stereo Tape Club of America in June 1971 for $4.2 million. Cerro terminated the operations of this business in 1972 and reported an extraordinary charge against earnings of some $.45 per share to provide for its losses. Also, Cerro in 1973 sold its 50 percent interest in Atlantic Cement for $38.5 million in cash. Thus far, it seems that Cerro is yet another conventional corporation going into retrenchment.

Actually, Cerro already owned a home builder, a real estate developer, a truck line, and a few joint venture participations in natural resources. Far from retrenching, Cerro, since the Stereo Tape fiasco and the sale of Atlantic Cement, has made these additional aggressive moves: negotiated to acquire a developer of shopping centers, entered into a joint venture in Europe to make and sell industrial service tubes to the air-conditioning and refrigeration industry, and bought 37.5 percent of Golconda Corp. from the troubled Westgate-California Corp.

Repurchasing of Stock

Toward the end of 1972 and in 1973 and 1974, there was another instance of the recurring pattern of publicly held corporations repurchasing their own stock. In fact, their repurchases exceeded $2 billion.

One can use this situation to support a case either for or against the validity of my concept of supercorporations. It can be argued that the collective rebuying of tens of millions of shares of the stocks of hundreds of publicly held corporations represents a retrenching, a cutting back, and therefore a tendency against building a super business empire. Or it can be argued that this repurchasing fever is a future-growth move for many corporations and an aggressive move toward super status for a few (aggressive in the sense that the corporations are accumulating inventories of their own stocks that will be useful in acquisitions and mergers and in compensating their growth-oriented executives).

An exploration of these massive stock repurchases will allow us to determine their relationship to the emergence of supercorporations. The inside reasons for repurchases are several. There are, in fact, long-recognized advantages of suitable, well-timed purchases and few disadvantages. The common advantages are, often, more productive use of excess cash, increased effectiveness in the use of corporate capital, an arithmetic increase (or a lesser decrease) in the repurchaser's earnings per share, and, sometimes, an advantage in financial relations. Also, in the event of a feared attack on a corporation, its management can help to defend it against a tender offer or some other form of raid by heavy repurchasing of the company's stock. One disadvantage, often embarrassing to management, is a further decline in the company's stock price after millions were spent to buy it back at an already depressed price.

As we would expect of any action of large corporations in the post-industrial society, the business of repurchasing one's own corporate stock is more complex than this brief sketch of it. In real life, though, the net advantages are quite enticing, and supercorporations are likely to be involved in their share of the action.

Ultimately, then, this array of repurchase motives makes clear that more is involved in repurchasing stock than merely corporate retrenchment or corporate aggressiveness. It is also evident that repurchasing is not the captive tool of any one type of company. Consequently, our third objection to the forecast coming of supercorporations is not a real objection at all.

Sufficiency of Raw Materials

This objection to the plausibility of supercorporations can be answered very quickly. There is, indeed, a sufficient number of billion-dollar corporations to supply the supers of the future. The 1974 *Fortune* Double 500 Directory listed 177 U.S. industrial corporations with 1973 sales or assets of a billion dollars or more. In addition, there were 37 diversified finance companies, 15 transportation companies, 27 retailing companies, and 35 life insurance companies—all with either gross revenues or assets of at least a billion dollars.

This inventory of almost 300 corporate candidates for super status excludes commercial banks and utilities because their regulatory situations would make a supercorporation effort impossible for them. Also excluded for the moment are the 144 foreign companies with assets or sales equivalent to a billion dollars or more. These require further study because of the different societies, economies, and traditions involved. A further exclusion from the present inventory of candidates for super status are at least a dozen of the strongest comers in the United States, corporations with sales of half a billion to a billion dollars. Some of these may prove to be superior prospects for super status, but our focus, you will recall, is not on identifying all the candidates.

Multinationals Versus Supercorporations

The fifth objection to the concept of supercorporations is that, at base, "supercorporation" is simply another name for the much attacked multinational corporation, and therefore supers are nothing new at all.

What are the differences, if any? In reality, three differences are discernible today: diversification, growth, and focus.

As to diversification, many multinationals, such as the integrated petroleums operating in many countries and the very large banks, are mainly one-industry companies. Thus, they have nowhere near the range of diversity that distinguishes a supercorporation. Exxon, First National City Bank, First National Bank of Chicago, Gulf, Mobil, and Texaco are true multinationals, but they are not supercorporations at all. As to growth, we require any corporation that could be called super to have double the average growth rate—10 percent per year compounded growth in earnings per share. Some very strong multinationals have not shown such growth and are, therefore, by definition not yet supercorporations. A random selection of major multinational companies with growth rates considerably below the required rates for supercorporations includes Borden, Celanese, Du Pont, W. R. Grace, Singer, and Union Carbide.

In addition to these two differences between multinationals and supers, the essential focus of a multinational will usually be different from that of a supercorporation.

The phrase "multinational corporation" emphasizes where this kind of giant operates but tells us little else about the company. For example, the joining together of Dunlop Holdings, Ltd., of England and Pirelli of Italy in 1971 was announced as a strong step forward because it produced a much more multinational company, among other things. By 1972–1973, however, there were widely reported difficulties in the union of the two famous tire makers, and they arranged to be partly unhooked from each other. Multinational, yes; supercorporation, no.

Both concepts—of multinationals and of supercorporations—are useful in understanding the impact of concentrated corporate power on business as a whole, on the economy, and on the society. Some multinationals have been so for a long time—for instance, Singer, for about a hundred years. Supercorporations will just begin to appear in the next few years. It would be of doubtful value to allow the mounting attacks on multinationals to obscure consideration of another protean movement—the development of the supercorporation. The next chapter, with an additional description of the supers, will put greater distance between most multinationals and most supercorporations.

We have seen that the five challenges to the notion of supercorporations are not effective. First, antitrust, in the United States and the European Common Market, will hurt and delay the supers, but it will not stop them any more than it has stopped ITT. Next, the widespread retrenchment by hundreds of conventional corporations, the cutting out of unrelated and unsuccessful diversifications, will continue. But it will not prevent up to several dozen of the most able and aggressive conventional managements from metamorphosing their corporations into supers. In a few cases, the retrenchment is an essential phase of putting a conventional corporation into condition to join the super race.

The repurchasing by corporations of more than $2 billion of their own stock could be misinterpreted as contrary to the supercorporation trend. But these repurchases are made for a variety of internal reasons and will neither abet nor deter the historical forces moving some corporations into super status.

Finally, well over 200 corporations in the United States are already of sufficient size to qualify as a base for a supercorporation. Although many of these billion-dollar companies are multinational in scope, we must be careful not to confuse multinationals with supers. They are two different breeds. Supers will be more diversified, grow faster, and have a different focus than most multinationals. Most multinationals will not become supercorporations. Some supers, however, will be multinational as well. Thus, we need to avoid thinking that the supers are already here, in the clothing of multinationals. Supers are not here yet. It will require great efforts to create them, and they will be visibly different from all other types of corporations.

The foregoing five objections answered, it is time to look at more of the evidence that supercorporations are actually on their way into our business world.

5

THE BEGINNINGS of the SUPERCORPORATIONS

IT IS ONE THING TO SAY that supercorporations will not be stopped before they start by antitrust or other opposing forces. That is negative evidence. But it is quite another thing to show that a previously unknown species of giant, with a brand-new name, is indeed going to appear in our midst in the 1970s and 1980s. The task is uncommon, because a genuinely new kind of corporation is a rarity.

The difficulty of the task, as you will see, is principally in getting recognition of the existing masses of facts and predictors. Plain evidence has been accumulating under our noses for most of the postwar years, especially during the later 1960s and early 1970s. If we can only sort out and accept what we already know, then we can recognize the shadow which the supercorporations are casting before themselves. We can also foresee their actual appearance, probably beginning in the late 1970s. Working over the evidence of supers that has been piling up will give us three interlocking indicators of their arrival.

First, however, we must deal with what I have called the fad syndrome in American business and with the impact of the scores of offshoots from the world of supercorporations that we are calling semisupers. There will also be many super effects infecting conventional corporations, thus rendering them more aggressive and productive.

The corporate fad syndrome is the collection of symptomatic tendencies in most American businessmen to follow the leader. Of the countless examples of follow-the-leader, we will use three as representative. In security analysis, if one report says that nursing homes, or airlines, or toy companies, or retailers are hot (or out of favor), then nearly all reports will say just about the same thing. In architecture, if one luxury apartment features the Mies van der Rohe style of stilts at the front of the building, then building after building in town will rise on stilts. In corporate communications, if a few companies adopt new symbols, then followers by the hundreds jump on that bandwagon, too. You probably have begun to supply your own examples while reading this list.

The fad syndrome can be expected to seize upon the idea of the supercorporation in the next several years, say by 1977 or 1978. By that time, it is likely that the first two or three supers will have emerged and will have been recognized as such. Then the rush will be on for many more companies to be recognized as supers, since it will have become an ''in'' thing to be. Do not underestimate the significance of the fad syndrome as we evolve into the world of supers. On the basis of past form, we can expect a lot of officers and directors to get interested in ''doing something'' about supercorporations, and ''doing something'' is likely to mean emulation. More aggressiveness. More resourcefulness. Finally kicking out some profitless businesses that have been hanging around for years. These officers will want a lot more bang for the buck when they create and use corporate capital. They will certainly try out some of the newer ideas that the supers will be making prominent.

It is impossible to predict whether the supers themselves or the host of their followers will have the greater impact on business and society by the 1980s. A case could be made either way. Either the supers will be the chief influence on us because of their size, prominence, and leadership, or perhaps five times as many other corporations—the semisupers—all hustling to adopt some super characteristics, will collectively have a greater effect. Or possibly hundreds of partly infected conventional corporations will do more to alter the corporate world and its effects on us. The supers, the semisupers, and other followers will indeed move us, by the year 1990, far from where we are at the present time.

Not knowing whether the genuine supers or their emulators will ultimately carry more weight, I have stuck to discussing the real supercorporations because they represent a clearer concept than do the semisupers or the camp followers. Along the way, to remind you of the possibly great importance of the semisupers and other followers I occasionally refer to them.

With this preamble, we are ready for the three kinds of evidence that foretell the coming of supercorporations and their effects.

The first evidence that supercorporations are already en route is the surprising persistence of conglomerate spirit and practice. These, as we have seen, represent one of the two parents of the supers (the other parent being some of the more aggressive and astute conventional corporations).

The second body of evidence of the coming supercorporations consists of the new moves that many conventional corporations are already making as they adopt some of the tactics and methods of conglomerates.

The third body of evidence is to be gleaned from a more detailed look at some possible future supers. Part One closes, therefore, with a comparison of the already visible super characteristics of two corporations with my definition of a supercorporation. The similarity, while not yet complete, is remarkable, and it foreshadows the full evolution of the supers.

The Living Conglomerates

The first category of evidence supporting the arrival of the supers is the previously unpredicted staying power of the conglomerate idea of the 1960s. This staying power, manifested in both conglomerate companies and in conglomerate ideas, is one of the essential ingredients of supercorporations.

It seems, in this instance, that almost nothing succeeds like failure. A previous section reviewed the abysmal fall of such high flyers as Boise Cascade, Whittaker, Republic, Litton, Ling-Temco-Vought, and others. But some of the conglomerates have recovered well. This indicates that there can be underlying soundness and growth, given good management and less hokum. Table 2 shows Gulf + Western's record, with its peak in 1969, its sharp decline in 1970, and its new high set in 1973. The residual strengths of some of the swinging conglomerates are a reason for the expanding penetration of conglomerate ideas into the conventional corporate consciousness.

Table 2.   Selected operating results of Gulf + Western Industries, Inc., for years ended July 31.

	1973	1972	1971	1970	1969
Gross revenues ($000)	$1,927,165	$1,669,671	$1,566,327	$1,629,562	$1,563,564
Net profits ($000)	89,351	69,601	55,252	44,771	72,050
Earnings per share, fully diluted	4.06	3.31	2.61	2.00	3.15

In addition to the continued and contagious vitality of some 1960 conglomerates, we find still another unpredicted form of vigorous conglomerate life in the apparently successful building of new conglomerates since the original swingers began to falter. Two cases in point are Fuqua Industries, formed in 1965, with most of its growth coming in 1968 and since; and Katy Industries, Inc., formed in 1970. A capsule review of these two new conglomerates will further confirm the virulence of conglomerate ideas and their permeating appeal to businessmen and the financial community.

Fuqua Industries began in September 1965, when J. B. Fuqua acquired control of a foundering company, National Fireproofing. He restored its profitability in 1966 and renamed it Fuqua Industries in 1967. Early acquisitions boosted sales in 1967 to $60 million. By 1968, when we saw that some older conglomerates were in deep trouble, Fuqua Industries spurted to sales of $200 million. The original company, now called Natco, was spun off in the same year.

All together, in about eight years, this newer swinging conglomerate acquired over 40 companies, sold off four of them, got into several joint ventures, built a financial structure of seven different debt and equity components, and had roller-coaster ups and downs in the price of its common stock. By 1973, sales were $479 million and profits $16.5 million. For 1974 management predicted sales of $541 million and profits of $24 million. Does this sound like the mid-1960s instead of the early 1970s? Indeed it does.

The second new conglomerate was formed in 1970 when the long-established American Gage & Machine Co. merged into, and took control of, the foundering Missouri-Kansas-Texas Railroad. Katy Industries is now in supermarkets, gas pipelines, frozen shrimp, electrical equipment, and a marine towing company, among other fields. From gross revenues of $67 million and a net loss of $6 million in 1969, Katy had grown by 1973 to gross revenues of nearly $188 million and profits of more than $12 million.

The Broadening of Conventional Corporations

The second parent of the supercorporations has already been acknowledged: some of the larger, more aggressive, better managed conventional corporations. Are they—any of them—likely parents? Can they, and might they, wed the beckoning conglomerate concept and tactics and produce super offspring?

Certain widely published bits and pieces of news on conventional corporations have never before been recognized as parts of a pattern. This pattern, now seen, features rampant diversification, increasingly complex financial structures, accelerated divestments, and unusual deals. Nearly the whole panoply of the 1960 conglomerates is already being adopted by an increasing number of conventional corporations.

All this is taking place right before our eyes, with the legally required public disclosures. Everyone has seen it, yet few have recognized it for what it is—a great change in our conventional corporations that loosens them from their conventional moorings and takes them further into some kind of conglomerate form.

We will examine this second evidence of the coming of the supers in several ways. First, a game, if you please—the familiar game of matching two separate columns. The Diversification Game provides a striking display of the increasing diversification of our decreasingly conventional corporations.

For each of the 20 conventional corporations listed with their basic business activities on the next pages, choose the field of diversification from the list that your knowledge tells you is the best match. (Note that the condensed listing of the present scope of conventional corporations alone tells us a lot about their increasingly swinging tendencies.) Place the number of the field you select beside the corporation's name. For example, if you think that Bath Industries has diversified into pleasure boats, place the number 2 in the space provided.

Fields of Diversification

1. Home furnishings
2. Pleasure boats
3. Toys
4. Garden supply stores
5. Heavy-duty tires
6. Venture capital financing and other financial services
7. Executive health care services
8. Insurance
9. Petroleum refining and marketing
10. High-performance materials
11. Jet aircraft
12. Food flavorings
13. Personal deodorants
14. Modular housing
15. Sprinkler systems
16. Moving pictures
17. Carpets
18. Limited-menu restaurants
19. Construction equipment
20. Miniature calculators

1. **Bath Industries, Inc.__**
   Naval and merchant ships.

2. **Beatrice Foods Co.__**
   Dairy, grocery, chemical, confectionery, and other products.

3. **Bethlehem Steel Corp.__**
   Basic and fabricated steel products, railroad products, shipbuilding, plastics, modular housing.

4. **Campbell Soup Co.__**
   Soups, spaghetti products, baked goods, and candies; frozen prepared foods; food service products; restaurant operations.

5. **Caterpillar Tractor Co.__**
   Earthmoving equipment and tractors, industrial and marine engines, forklift trucks.

6. **Control Data Corp.__**
   Computers, peripheral equipment, software, service bureaus, supplies.

7. **Dun & Bradstreet, Inc.__**
   Credit reports and other business information services, publishing, consulting services, marketing services, broadcasting.

8. **El Paso Natural Gas Co.__**
   Natural gas pipelines, petrochemicals, fibers and textiles, copper mining, manufacture of copper wire and cable.

9. **Esmark, Inc.** (formerly Swift & Co.)__
   Meat, dairy, poultry, and grocery products; edible oil; food services; engineering services; chemicals; leather; insurance agencies, underwriting.

10. **Exxon Corp.__**
Petroleum exploration, refining, and marketing; oceangoing tankers; pipelines; chemicals.

11. **Gates Rubber Co.__**
Molded rubber products for industrial applications, stereo tapes, industrial belting and hose products, auto tires.

12. **General Tire & Rubber Co.__**
Tires, chemicals, plastics, auto and appliance parts, other industrial components, broadcasting, air transport, CATV, aerospace.

13. **Greyhound Corp.__**
Bus and other transportation services; computer leasing; food products and services; aircraft and other services; insurance; car renting; money orders.

14. **Hercules Inc.__**
Naval stores, basic and intermediate chemicals (including those used in synthetic films and upholstery), optical scanning services for credit cards, paints, water treatment systems.

15. **INA Corp.__**
Property, casualty, and life insurance; investment banking and other financial services; health services; data processing services; residential and commercial development and commercial construction.

16. **Quaker Oats Co.__**
Breakfast cereals, pet food, toys, needlework products.

17. **RCA__**
Aerospace, defense, and other government contracting; vehicle renting; real estate services; television receivers, audio equipment; broadcasting; publishing; educational services; frozen prepared foods.

18. **Ralston Purina Co.__**
Breakfast cereals, soybeans, mushrooms, seafoods, and other food products; mariculture; pet foods, animal feed, and animal health products; resort operations; real estate development.

19. **Raytheon Co.__**
Defense systems, commercial electronics (including data handling systems and medical electronics), major appliances, engineering and construction services, educational publishing.

20. **Rockwell International__**
Aerospace and defense contracting, automotive products, civilian and military electronics, textile machinery, printing machinery, industrial components.

In some cases, the most congruent match is perfectly obvious: pleasure boats go to Bath Industries, heavy construction equipment to Caterpillar Tractor, more toys for Quaker Oats, and limited-menu restaurants for Campbell Soup. Some are less obvious but still create no surprise: synthetic-fiber carpets go to Hercules and heavy-duty tires go to Gates Rubber. The entire list can be matched in this way to indicate the continuing product and service diversification by the conventional companies listed.

Such a match would, at the same time, underscore the rapidly increasing degree of diversification of conventional corporations, which is one of our three categories of evidence that the supercorporation is coming and that, as a result of the historical forces that impel the supers, many conventional corporations will never be the same again. Never. In fact, by the late 1970s many of them may no longer be regarded as conventional corporations, but as semisupers. Of course, the public relations people will devise a name easier to huckster than semisuper, but the concept should be clear with our working title of semisuper.

If you have matched the fields of diversification to the corporations in that way, you have been logical—but all wrong. *All* wrong. The correct answers match up by number, which puts (1) Bath Industries in (1) home furnishings, (2) Beatrice Foods in (2) pleasure boats, and so on through the entire list until we have Rockwell International matched with—of all things—miniature calculators. INA Corp., once a staid property and casualty insurance company, owns the Star Sprinkler Co. In the face of such unrecognized diversifications, it is equally plausible for Bethlehem Steel to have acquired a toy business and for Hercules, Inc., the ninth largest chemicals corporation, to have entered modular housing. I especially like the idea of General Tire in the food flavoring business.

It does sound, well, conglomerate, doesn't it? It sounds that way because it is.

Nor, as we have seen, are these hitherto unpredicted and unrecognized conglomerate forms of diversification the only aspect of the sinking conventionalism of many nominally conventional corporations. Of several other conglomeratelike undertakings, two more need to be recognized: the increasing use of less than 100 percent owned ventures and the increasing complexity of the financial structures of once simply financed corporations. These changes, too, have been publicly announced and widely seen, but they have been observed as a pattern almost not at all.

Regarding less than 100 percent ownership, which as we saw was required by prudent operating policy, there are more and more holes in the dike. In 1970 the Carborundum Company formed a joint venture with Universal Grinding of Stafford, England. The new company, Universal Carborundum of Australia, Ltd., located in Melbourne, takes over and combines Australian businesses previously owned separately by the two joint venture parents. Another example is that of the Chase Manhattan Bank, which has teamed with Mitsubishi to form an extensive consulting and services enterprise for Asia. General Mills Inc. and Rhone-Poulenc S.A. have formed a joint venture through subsidiaries to produce xanthan gum, used in oil drilling operations. Three U.S. and one Canadian company have formed a unit to build a $250 million petrochemicals plant in Ontario.

Again, the evidence is extensive, and these examples are representative. Conventional corporations are increasingly throwing off the shackles of unnecessarily restrictive policies, and some of them are thereby adding more and more of the aspects of supercorporations.

In addition to joint ventures and partial ownerships at home, more U.S. conventional corporations are entering into arrangements of less than 100 percent ownership in foreign operations. Not surprisingly, two of the large U.S. auto companies have made multi-million-dollar investments in Japanese auto companies. General Motors has an interest in Isuzu and Chrysler in Mitsubishi Motors Corp. Also, International Harvester has acquired one-third interest in a new commercial vehicle manufacturing company formed by DAF of Eindhoven, Holland. Standard Brands has joint ventures in Brazil and three other Latin American countries, plus 15 joint-venture plants in Latin America and Europe. And Cities Service Co. has a 34.6 percent interest in a carbon black plant in India.

One other conglomerate practice being adopted in the name of conventional growth is the abandonment of the simplest financial structure for more complex structures as required by growth opportunities. "New" financial structures make it possible for the erstwhile conventional corporation to create more capital, or create it more desirably, than is feasible with the simplest structure (one class of common stock and sometimes some long-term debt). U.S. transportation companies, hotel chains, utilities, and some other corporations have normally used more complex financial structures, but this is the first such adventure for a growing aggregation of conventional corporations.

First, there was the tidal wave of debt financing by conventional U.S. corporations in Western Europe. This, to be sure, was a largely artificial condition, in that it was forced by U.S. efforts to stanch the outflow of dollars adversely affecting our balance of payments. Artificiality aside, these additional debt financings represent a different form of financing, and one that would not have been predicted for conventional U.S. corporations as recently as 20 years ago. The point is that the conventional corporations went ahead with out-of-policy financing and financial structure instead of pulling back, as their prudent policies would formerly have required.

Second, there has been a marked advance in the number of conventional U.S. corporations that have added one or more types of additional stock to their capital structure, especially in the past several years. The volume of preferred stock sold by corporations in 1969 was $682 million. In 1970 $1.3 billion; 1971, $3.6 billion; 1972, $3.2 billion. To say that this shift in financial structure is a natural response to changing conditions in the financial markets is true, but it is not the full story. Financial markets have always changed; the new situation is that more large corporations have been willing and able to respond to those changes by moving away from the customary very simple financial structures.

Third, as a further portent of the less conventional approach to financial structure, witness the large U.S. commercial banks. These institutions are not and will not be prospects for supercorporations. Their more adventurous financial structures are cited as a difference in the tone of management thinking generally. Federal and state laws and an abiding public sentiment against unlimited expansion and diversification by banks will continue to hem them in far short of supercorporate status. Still, their new financial structures, within their special legal limits, are a sign of a less conventional approach to financial structure throughout the entire U.S. business and financial community. Two already familiar financing actions of banks were, after all, generally unknown as recently as about a dozen years ago: the selling of long-term debt to the public and the formation of one-bank holding companies.

For nearly two centuries in the United States, bank capital usually consisted of capital stock and surplus. No debt. Banks loaned, they did not borrow in the financial markets. What could be more prudent, more conventional? Notwithstanding all this, the large central-city commercial banks began borrowing billions of dollars from the public in the 1960s, thereby expanding their capital structures and their capacity for further growth.

The other less than conventional change in financial structure was the nearly unanimous switch by the largest banks to one-bank holding company status, following federal enabling legislation. This arrangement involves first the creation of a new corporation, the holding company. The original business, the bank itself, becomes a wholly owned subsidiary of the new holding company. The new holding company is permitted by federal law to enter into certain businesses, specifically named and limited by the Comptroller of Currency, into which most banks had not previously entered. These businesses include, as of the middle of 1974, such financial services as mortgage banking, leasing, accounts-receivable financing, some management of funds, certain data processing services, small business investment companies, and real estate investment trusts.

So in a few years, and despite regulation, the large commercial banks of the country have metamorphosed from single corporations in one or a few businesses and with no debt to one-bank holding companies in up to eight or ten specified businesses and corporations and with billions of dollars in long-term debt, collectively. This situation, also, will not by itself bring in the supercorporations. But it is a further straw in the winds of unconventionality and experimentation with less than the simplest financial structures.

Two Prospective Supercorporations

The evidence that more and more conventional corporations are becoming something quite unconventional leads to the third and last part of the brief for supercorporations: two examples of a company developing into something tolerably close to a supercorporation. The first company is General Electric and the second is ITT. In presenting two potential supers, we must be clear on what is implied. I am not specifically predicting that either GE or ITT will become a supercorporation. It is too soon after the development of the concept of supercorporations to pick companies that are either likely or unlikely to achieve this new status. The purpose of the following sections is to substantiate further the whole concept of supers by showing how far GE and ITT have already progressed toward being supercorporations.

First, let us review the characteristics of a supercorporation:

1. Size of at least a billion dollars in sales or assets.

2. Extremely broad diversification into three, and usually more, fields not closely related to one another.

3. A high degree of flexibility, aggressiveness, resourcefulness, and creativity in operations, usually including efficient use of capital; rapid entry into, and exit from, new businesses and profit centers; partial ownership and other nonconventional forms of ventures; high rewards for key executives; and possibly some new approaches to handling people problems.

4. As a result, an average annual compound growth rate far higher than is achieved by most other large corporations—10 percent in earnings per common share. All the descriptives in this requirement are important, but "average" must be emphasized. The increase in earnings per share need not exceed 10 percent *every* year, and only an average of over 10 percent is required, allowing for some better years and some poorer years.

5. Usually, but not necessarily, a super will also be a multinational.

GENERAL ELECTRIC

General Electric more than meets the size and multinational criteria. In 1973, GE had sales of $11.6 billion and total assets of $8.3 billion. The company's international sales were $2.3 billion, involving operations in every significant area of the free world.

Requirement No. 2 is extremely broad diversification into three or more fields or industries. Rather than assuming that GE qualifies, let's look at the unconventional reach of GE's diversification.

GE is active in the following four fields in the United States (figures in parentheses represent 1973 sales): industrial components and systems ($3.7 billion), consumer products ($3.1 billion), industrial power equipment ($2.5 billion), and aerospace ($1.6 billion). Within each of these major fields, the scope of diversification is partly described by these examples:

—Industrial components and systems: Transportation systems, engineering plastics, batteries, computer time-sharing, industrial heating, medical systems, cutting tools.

—Consumer products: Air conditioners, broadcasting, light bulbs, stereo equipment, appliances and services, heat pumps.

—Industrial power equipment: Gas turbines, insulators, meters, nuclear power reactors and fuel, power circuit breakers, switch gears, steam turbine-generators.

—Aerospace: Aircraft jet engines, aerospace instruments, armament systems, missile reentry systems, radar, sonar.

In addition to its activity in these four widely disparate areas, GE is still further diversified with such enterprises as a venture capital company, Business Development Services, Inc.; the GE Credit Corp.; extensive royalty and technical agreements, which brought in $37 million of income in 1973; and the sale, to all comers, of the GE economic forecasting service.

Some conglomerates would be proud of the extent and scope of diversification achieved by General Electric. And we still classify it as a conventional corporation?

The next criterion is that of growth. GE's long-term growth rate has not as yet qualified it for the supercorporation category. During the last four ten-year periods reported in the 1974 *Fortune* Directory, GE's earnings-per-share growth has been well less than an average of 10 percent per year, compounded. *Forbes* calculated that GE's average annual growth rate for the five years ending in 1972 was 13.4 percent. This is the same period in which the more than 700 companies so measured had a median growth rate of only 3.6 percent. But, in the succeeding 1968–1973 period, *Forbes* assessed GE's average earnings-per-share growth to have been only 4.9 percent.

GE, with its outstanding management, active social commitments, excellent return on investment, and other valuable aspects, may or may not increase its growth rate as the world of supers takes form. If not, there would be two likely reasons. First, GE's $11.6 billion size may be too large to permit such rapid growth. We know that there are plenty of companies one-fifth to one-tenth the size of GE which can become supers without having to move the tremendous mass built by GE. Second, GE places such strong emphasis on a high return on investment—18 percent in 1972 and 1973—that this policy may preclude a super rate of growth.

The final criterion, not measurable by instant means, is that of aggressiveness, resourcefulness, flexibility, and creativity. The preceding description of GE, together with your own knowledge, should support GE's meeting this subjective and essential criterion. Whether or not GE becomes a full-fledged supercorporation, or even wants to, you can see how far one U.S. corporation has already gone in the direction I predict for one to two dozen other exceptionally well managed corporations.

ITT

Unfavorable publicity about an ITT antitrust settlement and other controversial ITT actions have led to concern about this company's large size and some of its methods. *The Sovereign State of ITT* is one expression of this concern.[1] One could conclude that if ITT is to become a supercorporation, with all the additional power and scope this status implies, then one might not welcome the emergence of supercorporations at all.

Such a conclusion is central to the concerns of this book. As supercorporations come into being, large questions of public policy arise. Will supers help to improve the business economy and the postindustrial society or will they be taking more than they give? Will there be more concerns about domestic and foreign political influence, as in U.S.-ITT antitrust proceedings, the ITT involvement in Chilean elections, and its influence in Ecuadorian expropriation settlements? Or will supercorporations and their emulators contribute to the "second American Revolution" as described by John D. Rockefeller III [2]?

Remember that a supercorporation will be a new type of corporation that is not merely larger but different in nature and quality. The differences may be good or ill, but differences there will be. Parts Two and Three of this book explore some of the concrete areas in which the supers might contribute valuably to the business community and to society generally, as a part of their probably rapid future growth.

With this slightly hopeful but wary perspective on supers, let us return to ITT as a prospective supercorporation.

As was the case with General Electric, ITT fulfills the criteria of a supercorporation to a high degree. ITT, with 1973 gross revenues of $10.2 billion, is already of supercorporation size. Its diversification is

---

[1] Anthony Simpson, New York, Stein & Day, 1973.
[2] *The Second American Revolution, Some Personal Observations* (New York, Harper & Row, 1973).

more than enough to qualify for super status. Its interests include cosmetics, telecommunications, insurance, baked goods, grass seed, hotels and motels, real estate development, industrial controls, electronic and electromechanical components, building materials, book publishing, and many more.

It is obvious that ITT is a wonder among very large corporations in terms of aggressiveness, flexibility, resourcefulness, and creativity—whether or not its application of these qualities is acceptable to you. Thus, we know that ITT has amply met three of the four requirements for supercorporation status, and it is a leading multinational company as well. Regarding the fourth mandatory characteristic, rapid growth, I have to withhold judgment. ITT earnings computations are so complex and murky that I suggest we await further evidence. Whether or not ITT becomes a supercorporation, it gives us another example of how close one corporation has already come and another indication of the probable arrival of a number of supercorporations by 1990.

GE and ITT are not the only potential supercorporations. Other companies are also evolving into this difficult-to-achieve status. The following ten companies are some early examples of potential supers (I am not making definite predictions as to which ones will or will not make it into the super circle): American Express, City Investing, Dow Chemical, Georgia-Pacific, INA Corporation, IU International Corp. (formerly International Utilities), 3M, Sears, Roebuck, Teledyne, and Westinghouse. This list should spark controversy. However, I hope it will also lead, with the other ideas in this book, to a tough evaluation of my prediction of a new kind of corporation with a high degree of impact.

One point before the sparks start flying: We must continue to distinguish between supers, which will grow fast, and the classic growth companies, which also grow fast. Thus, IBM, Xerox, Eastman Kodak, and other superb companies are left in their own special group. Relative to such growth companies, I emphasize that the supers will be more diversified, more oriented toward acquisition and new ventures, and more inclined toward unusual financial, ownership, and operational arrangements.

PART TWO

SUPERCORPORATIONS
and the
BUSINESS COMMUNITY

The art of progress is to preserve order amid
change and to preserve change amid order.
> —ALFRED NORTH WHITEHEAD

The collision of supercorporations with our workaday world will scramble nearly everything we do in business, from the one-man storefront to the federal establishment, from the mundane organization chart to the exotica of corporate consciousness-raising.

A Closer Look at Supers

Part One suggested that the supercorporation, a very different kind of corporation, is evolving out of a combination of some large conventional corporations with some of the adventurous methods of the 1960 conglomerates. It also showed that the internal realities of corporate life will have a lot to do with this curious evolution. Beyond the vital externals of the postindustrial society—its national and world economics, technology, social change, and the like—something coursing in the corporate bloodstream is propelling a few large conventional corporations into a very different state of being.

Part Two attempts, by means of a closer look at the business nature of the supercorporation, to predict the effects of the supers on U.S. businesses, business people, and those with whom they deal. It speaks most to corporate executives and employees in both the supercorporations-to-be and the large and small companies that must compete, deal, or just coexist with the supers. But it also has messages for government officials, critics of the business system, and students of business.

For business people, there are constructions of the possible effects of supercorporations on their business lives, including the way their companies may be organized at the top; the probable adoption of a wide-ranging new function, venture management; and further attempts at improving the management of people in business. Businessmen will also be forewarned in Part Two about a new set of customer-supplier relationships that will lead to much wider use of another entity, the "multiple captive."

Attorneys, trade associations, and the trade publication field, among many others, will find their worlds permanently changed by the development of supers, and the supercorporation will impact nearly all other service professions, businesses, and institutions as well.

Of special interest to government officials and others dealing with the business community, Part Two projects a different type and timbre of competition between supers and other businesses. Students and critics of the business system will find the possibility of new life in this much-criticized system.

A note, again, on the use of language. For directness and ease of reading, we are saying that supercorporations will come and will do all manner of things to us. For ''will'' please continue to read ''probably will,'' for no futurist can guarantee the future.

Supercorporations Versus the 1960 Conglomerates

Although I predict that the emerging supercorporations will aggressively use certain methods of the 1960 conglomerates, they will become a very different type of business enterprise. Let us look at the gross differences between the two categories of conglomerates.

The swinging conglomerates of the 1960s (1) were usually slapped together on the back of a small, underfinanced company, (2) were put together largely with rapid-fire acquisitions and mergers, (3) relied heavily for expansion capital on their high stock prices and price-earnings multiples (which reached 40 to 70 at their peak), and (4) mustered little resistance to extreme declines in earnings.

The supercorporations, however, will (1) be founded on billion-dollar blue-chip corporations or other major corporate bases, (2) rely considerably more than the 1960 conglomerates on internal growth and resources, (3) be better financed and less promotional in the stock and other financial markets, and (4) have an unusual amalgam of downside stability and rapid growth.

The following list further spells out the differences between the swinging conglomerates and the supercorporations:

Characteristic	1960 Conglomerates	Supercorporations
Beginning size	Small, $2 million to $50 million in annual sales. (G + W was originally an auto bumper factory in Michigan selling $2 million per year.)	Large, with a minimum of about a billion dollars in sales or assets.
Beginning capital	Small, in the range of $10 million or less. (Litton began with capital of under $5 million.) Initially, little	Large, since sales or assets are required to be a billion dollars or more. Large potential for further expand-

Characteristic	1960 Conglomerates	Supercorporations
	stock-market or other financial acceptance.	ing their capital in worldwide financial markets.
Pace of acquisitions and other external ventures	Rapid. (G + W acquired 49 companies in one year.)	Moderate. Probably two to four significant external ventures per year.
Proportion of internal growth to total growth	Hard to measure; claimed to be high, but probably low.	High. Existing billiondollar bases will provide much of the supers' growth.
Degree of diversification	Extreme. (The hundreds of companies owned by Alco Standard are in dozens of different industries, and many have no relationship to one another.)	From substantial to almost as extreme as that of the swingers. Each super will be in three or more different industries, and there may not be strong operating relationships among them.
Managerial and financial strategy	Overwhelming emphasis on rapid, uninterrupted growth for as long as possible, with little attention to managing the business.	Strong emphasis on above-average growth, with concentration on fewer, larger, and more thoroughly developed ventures and with comprehensive planning, direction, and control.
Promotional posture	Insistent to the point of being fictional.	Aggressive but sound and defensible.
Price-earnings multiples	40 to 70 or more at their all-time highs; now 5 to 16.	Probably above the Dow Jones Industrial Average, and equal to or above the current multiples of the 1960 conglomerates. (GE has sold at 23 times earnings, Sears, Roebuck at 29 times, when Dow Jones Industrials were selling at 15–17 times earnings.)
Quality of management and key staff	Hard to measure, but appeared to be very thin; many of the original managers have since left.	Substantial; comparable to that of the best conventional corporations.

Let us now proceed to explore a series of conceivable effects of supercorporations on the business community and on individual businesses. There are three categories of impact: on competition, on internal corporate operations, and on managers' business lives.

6

SUPERCORPORATIONS and COMPETITION

COMPETITION IS A fragile and elusive phenomenon that suffers from the lack of common understanding of what it is, how it is recognized and measured, and how it is supported or undermined. Nevertheless the U.S. businessman finds himself in demanding competition with both foreign and domestic companies. Because supercorporations will be both large and strikingly different kinds of businesses, their possible effects on existing patterns of competition require some imaginative forethought.

However, a crevasse of misunderstanding and disagreement should be charted before we proceed. That crevasse divides the traditional American conception of genuine, if circumscribed, competition from the view of some people that competition just does not exist at all. These people are numerous and intelligent, and some are highly placed in business and government, here and abroad. Those who see little or no business competition include a body of U.S. economists and sociologists; some U.S. politicians and voters; some antiestablishment rebels, who may or may not belong to either of the foregoing categories; some foreign business executives, including Europeans and Japanese; and at least one high official of the European Economic Community.

All these people believe that the "myth" of U.S. competition is either ingeniously or ingenuously palmed off on the American public, much of which swallows this tall tale whole. The implications of this viewpoint are serious for supercorporations, great for the business community, and possibly cataclysmic in our attempts to connect a partially free-market economy at home with effective trade and monetary performance abroad.

Before ruminating on these implications, let a well-placed European economist state the case for those who deny the very existence of competition in American business. Pierre Malve, a key policy aide of the Commission of the European Communities in Brussels, states unequivocally: "Certain taboos must be renounced, like the myth of free enterprise." [1] The myth of free enterprise is misleading, he says, for it "largely disregards the economic reality characterized by public subsidies and government controls" in the United States and other Atlantic Community democracies.

Hear also Masao Kanno, vice chairman of the Japanese Business Advisory Committee to the Organization for Economic Cooperation and Development: "It seems to me the beautiful bird of freedom [of competition] has flown away, and she will never come back again." [2] That is pretty strong stuff.

Is competition a myth or a beautiful bird that has flown away forever? No. Neither domestic observers nor foreign business executives, nor others, will convince White Motor Corp., which lost much of its domestic market share in the years before 1971, that competition is anything but one of the most brutal facts of business life. The same is true for the supermarket industry, which was mauled by a price war in 1972 and 1973. Other true believers that competition lives are the regulated U.S. airlines, such as Pan American, which lost, and TWA, which won, a battle for passengers on what was once a highly profitable route for Pan Am.

A final group of examples takes in the advertising media. The three television networks really believe that they compete with one another, with CATV, and with newspapers, magazines, and other media. In fact, a quaintly worded dismissal of the existence of competition does not deal with the deaths of dozens of magazines, including *Life, Look, The Saturday Evening Post, Collier's, Liberty,* and *The American Magazine.* Has the bird of competition flown away? What do you think?

[1] Quoted in Richard F. Janssen, *The Wall Street Journal* (January 29, 1973), p. 1.
[2] Ibid.

This is not the place for answering all the arguments that business competition does not exist. The few examples just cited are, in fact, typical of what seems to be going on in large segments of the U.S. domestic business community, as well as what many top managers and boards of directors perceive to be going on. As we observed in Part One, the increasingly active antitrust "industry" in this country is doing more about defending and beefing up the existing state of competition.

Whether or not you believe in it, the day-to-day fact of competition in the postindustrial American economy is an assumption of this book, and this assumption leads to a concerned consideration of supercorporations and their probable good and bad effects on that competition.

Actually, as I see it, supercorporations may affect business competition in four ways, mostly unexpected: first, in terms of price competition and competition in innovation; second, in customer-supplier relationships; third, with respect to make-versus-buy decisions; and fourth, in the creation of many more "multiple captives."

Competition in Pricing and Innovation

Price competition of the direct, combative, price-cutting variety, such as retail price wars, is unlikely to be a frequent product of the supers. This form of price competition is, if anything, likely to decrease as a result of the different character of business operations of supercorporations. Antitrust proponents are, however, invited to stay for the full discussion before summarily deciding to strike against supers as an anticompetitive force.

Head-on price-cutting competition generically centers in commodities and in other products only slightly differentiated in the buyer's mind. Price wars have been familiar over gasoline, lumber, plywood, some items sold in retail stores, wholesale drugs, bulk chemicals, aluminum, cement, greige goods, and so on.

It is unlikely that supercorporations, which will grow at far above average rates, will seek to enter or expand into price-cut commodities, products, and services. Aside from boom times and artificial shortages, the price-cutting segments of the business world have shown both low rates of profitability and low growth in profits. The strategy of supercorporations will more likely be to avoid entering fields that engender toe-to-toe pricing slugfests and to get out of those highly price-competitive fields that may have been inherited from their conventional pasts. One route out of price-destructive "profit" centers is, of course, divestment or liquidation. Part One viewed the increasing willingness of even conventional corporations to admit their mistakes publicly and to cut their losses by opting out. Supers will do more along those lines.

Another way out of cutthroat price competition for the supers is product or service development, improvement, or replacement. Here the supers will shine, and their superiority will lead to competition in terms of innovation and enhanced values. This tendency, far from being a Pollyanna dream, comes right out of classical economic theory: the producer seeks to differentiate his product in order to establish a "monopoly" position. This sterile-sounding economic theory takes on substance as one sees the profitable innovations created by conventional corporations. In the household, the commoditylike sad irons of yore have been replaced by electric, self-cleaning, thermostatically controlled, lightweight steam irons. In industry low-yielding disease-prone seed stocks have been dropped, or hybridized into far greater productivity—and strong profits—for the hybridizers.

Customer-Supplier Relationships

The next effect of supercorporations on competition is likely to be in customer-supplier relationships. There are two principal cases: the super as the customer of the small- and medium-size business and the super as the supplier. The emerging supercorporations will be more rational customers of smaller conventional corporations, rational in the sense that they are likely to be tougher taskmasters, concentrating their purchasing with those smaller companies that are more reliable, prompt, and consistent in quality and services. This is good news for some purveyors to supers and bad news for others.

Another aspect of the supers' purchasing rationality is the greater prospect of profits and stability. Does this seem improbable because the purchaser will be a giant that can pound down the prices it pays? It is likely nonetheless, although this is not an answer to satisfy the doubters. Large conventional corporations have evolved a more enlightened purchasing ethic, especially since World War II, and this may be toned up by the new supercorporations. No longer is being a supplier to a giant a one-way ticket to a quick boom and certain doom, as the giant first bloats its orders and then cuts them off peremptorily. Johnson & Johnson, which has a leading growth record, is one of the large corporations whose executives have given me indications of a longer range, constructive set of relationships with suppliers, including small ones.

The relationship between the smaller supplier and the gargantuan purchaser may thus be a healthy one for some small businessmen, and may provide a fillip to more bracing competition in U.S. industry. It will not be a security blanket, but it will be a decent game to play.

Reversing the players, consider the supercorporation as a supplier and the resulting effects on competition. In many cases, the super may be competing directly with smaller companies as a supplier to other companies. To the extent that the supers enhance the level of products and services, the purchasers are directly benefited, and competition is ultimately strengthened, both at the supplier stage and through the resulting improvement in the customer's efficacy. One case from the services will corroborate this apparently golden idealism with results familiar to most of you who buy insurance for your automobiles.

The property and casualty insurance industry was characterized for decades by a few large companies and hundreds of small ones selling primarily through independent agents, who received commissions of 25 percent on rather high-priced auto insurance policies. Whether it appears idealistic or not, Sears, Roebuck's Allstate Insurance Co. has become one of the largest auto insurers, with substantially lower prices, lower marketing costs, and very competitive service. Allstate even made profits during periods when some of its higher priced competitors were losing hundreds of millions of dollars every year on their auto policies.

Aside from the values of its campaigns for highway safety and better built cars, Allstate has introduced greater economic efficiency into a multi-billion-dollar industry. Other companies have performed similarly, but Allstate's example is familiar to those who may question the value to competition of a giant flexing its muscles among small- and medium-size competitors. Again, the supercorporation as a supplier will alter and intensify competition, but may leave competition as vigorous as before, if not more so.

Make-Versus-Buy Decisions

One of the shocking effects of supercorporations on competition will be a broader and more analytical handling of make-versus-buy decisions. The whole complex of dealing with giant corporations will be shatteringly changed by the supers' different way of evaluating and using the services and products they need.

In some cases the supers will decide to stop providing some of their own products or services and to go into the marketplace, thus opening up that much more purchasing power to the competitive market. In opposite cases, the supers will deem it profitable to stop buying some products and services, and to begin supplying themselves, effectively removing those items from competition.

This extension of a familiar business procedure can affect, for good or ill, perhaps a half million corporations that now supply or could supply large companies, plus hundreds of thousands of unincorporated service establishments and professional people. The vast service industries will be much harder hit by this sort of action on the part of the supers than the products sector of the economy. The reason is that large corporations have for decades looked closely at decisions to make or buy products related to their own, but have been conditioned by convention to stay out of many service industries that are less related to their own natural fields of interest.

A review of the sphere of make-versus-buy will put a new light on the way hundreds of thousands of corporations, individual businesses, and professional practices will function in the coming world of the supercorporation. Moreover, the supers will have a multiplier effect on the millions of employees of these supplier businesses, their principals, and the families involved. For brevity, this subject will be treated almost entirely in terms of service groups. You can easily entertain the same line of thinking regarding supercorporations and the companies that supply them with products.

"The service groups" is a blanket phrase that covers hundreds of different types of services, including professional services. To name only some of them, the service groups include accountants; attorneys; architects and engineers; commercial bankers; investment bankers; appraisers; contractors of a dozen types; advertising, public relations, and financial relations specialists; consulting actuaries; industrial and other realtors; management consultants of all imaginable varieties;

maintenance and repair services for office and other equipment; truck lines and other transportation services; interior decorators and art counselors and dealers; trade associations; trade publications; contract-service groups for computer facilities management and computer service bureaus; leased-department operators; food service companies; investment advisers and fund managers; leasing companies; and insurance carriers, agents, consultants, and brokers. (Trade associations, trade publications, and professional services are treated in separate sections below.)

This intentionally lengthy listing suggests the perhaps 10 to 20 million individuals in service fields dealing with the business community in the United States. It also suggests the range of people likely to feel the effects of supercorporations personally. With variations depending on the kind of service, the general scope of the supers' effects on service groups will most probably include: (1) more stringent make-versus-buy decisions, with more "make" in some fields than in the past; (2) palpably tighter performance requirements and scrutiny of costs and expenses; and (3) outright elimination of certain services, including some that have been used for 50 to 100 years. Supercorporations will all be very large entities, and in principle it will be more economical for them to provide more of their own services, simply through the economies of scale. That factor is certainly common to all other types of large corporations.

Another basis for supers' deciding to provide more of their own services is the far wider range of businesses that the supers will permit themselves to enter. Using another example from a conventional corporation to help peer into the future, 1973 saw a utility committing millions to go into the tanker business. In make-versus-buy language, the utility is edging closer to "making" its own transportation service, instead of buying its transportation as most utilities have done most of the time for the last hundred years. A subsidiary of Pacific Lighting Corp. of Los Angeles granted a $2.5 million contract to Sun Shipbuilding and Dry Dock Co. for a study of tanker design. Pacific Lighting has also taken an option to buy five tankers for $100 million each—a total of half a billion dollars' worth of tankers. The tankers, if Pacific Lighting buys them, would haul liquefied natural gas from Alaska and Indonesia to Southern California. If one of the less venturesome types of conventional corporations, the utility, can set itself up to "make" its own transportation service, there ought to be some breathtaking reaches by supercorporations into services that they used to buy when they were acting as conventional corporations.

The second respect in which supercorporations will affect make-versus-buy decisions on services will be in tighter performance requirements and greater scrutiny of costs and expenses. Some regulated companies pay legal fees of more than a million dollars a year. One conglomerate has paid out over a half million dollars in fees to have experts straighten out the grab bag of pension plans that was collected during its acquisition binge of the late 1950s and the 1960s. Such large amounts of service fees and charges have been little considered by conventional corporations, growth companies, or conglomerates. On the other hand, most of these companies for years have had a limitation of $25,000 to $100,000 on capital (that is, product) expenditures. Any larger expenditures must be approved by top management, and sometimes by the board of directors or one of its committees, while lower level managers have bought much larger amounts of services with little supervision or review.

As the conventional corporations go, so will the supers, but more so. For example one $2 billion conventional corporation in consumer products decided to take a hard look at its fee payments for executive recruiting. This company found that it was paying over $500,000 per year in executive recruiting and other personnel-finding fees to outside groups.

This corporation still uses ("buys") executive recruiting services, but it has changed the whole ball game by "making" more of its own recruiting services and by tightening down on the remaining service suppliers. The company insists that it is filling the positions that need to be filled from the outside, and that the quality and speed of hires have been satisfactory. The dollar results are instructive. In only two years, the company has reduced its recruiting cost per new employee from between $4,000 and $5,000 to about $1,300. In total, these costs have been reduced by hundreds of thousands of dollars per year.

So much for tighter performance requirements and increased scrutiny of costs and expenses as a part of intensified work on make-versus-buy decisions. Supercorporations, with more demanding growth targets than most conventional corporations, should be capable of tightening the thumbscrew on all corporate services.

The third way in which supercorporations can be expected to deal with make-versus-buy decisions regarding hundreds of different types of services will be to eliminate some of these services. Little has been published on the permanent elimination of services by the customer, since he has no wish to add insult to injury. In the large and lush insurance industry, there has been much talk and a modicum of action aimed at eliminating the service of insurance agents or brokers as it has existed in this country for nearly 200 years. Insurance agents and brokers alone, aside from the insurance companies, represent a multi-billion-dollar industry. Just the commercial side of it employs tens of thousands, and this is in addition to the large personal insurance business.

The possibility of the elimination of the brokerage and agency service (not the insurance itself) was raised by conventional corporations before the days of supercorporations and will be carried forward further and faster by the supers. Some of the alternatives started by conventional corporations that will be expanded by supers, semisupers, and their followers are the use of consultants whose costs will be lower than those of agents; the use of captive agencies and captive insurance companies, both domestic and offshore; and more elaborate self-insurance.

Please bear in mind that the insurance industry is not alone the object of supers' make-versus-buy decisions and other growth efforts. Insurance is used as a frequent example only as a convenience because it is familiar to most readers. Other areas, perhaps less familiar, that will also be threatened with elimination include certain routine and human aspects of product and process design services, to be replaced by high-speed computer-assisted drawing and plotting; some psychological testing and evaluation services, after findings of insufficient correlations of subsequent achievements with the original psychological evaluations; architectural and many engineering services in the construction of buildings, through the use of standard designs, drawings, components, and equipment; and quantities of elaborate, custom-designed computer software, through the use of extremely powerful general retrieval systems which provide many of the same answers from the computer as do the more expensive and specially written programs.

SOME SPECIFIC EFFECTS OF SUPERCORPORATE FALLOUT

The explosive effects of supercorporations, followed by other postindustrial corporations, on nearly all services and product businesses will be so great that we ought to examine a few examples. A futurist view of supers acting on dental services, trade associations, and trade publications should tell the story also about all the rest of the professionals and companies that will be changed far more than they have imagined.

Dentists—professionals in the supercorporate climate. Many large corporations, including the supers, will find themselves providing very expensive dental plans for employees and their families. Proposals for such plans to date usually involve adding specified dental services to a prepaid plan such as Blue Shield, with an increase over the previous Blue Shield fees.

Our first reaction to this increase in funds and demand for dental services is an expectation that dentists' fees will go up. This kind of effect has been reported in some physicians' fees after the introduction of Medicare and Medicaid.

However, the result of large corporate purchases or sponsorship of services will not necessarily be a further hypodermic to otherwise rising fee levels. Instead, two effects are to be watched for: first, a strong counterpressure against increases in fee levels; second, leadership and help toward more efficient delivery systems. The fundamental contribution of the supercorporations to the purchasing of services—dental and many others—will not be a result merely of their billion-dollar or larger size. It will come from their characteristic combination of aggressiveness and flexibility. There will be fewer sacred cows, whether in dental societies or in corporate boardrooms.

Regarding dental societies, some supers might take a direct stand against fee levels that are considered excessive. If this seems too unbusinesslike, remember that a leading insurance company, the Allstate subsidiary of Sears, Roebuck, has been making slashing attacks against shoddy auto construction. That was not predicted by businessmen or business observers before it happened. We must get used to the idea that at least a few big companies having some of the characteristics of supers are going to be as strident in standing for a cause as Allstate's television commercials have been in showing hundreds of dollars' worth of unnecessary car repairs from five-mile-per-hour crashes.

Hopefully, a more constructive supercorporation approach to securing better values for the company's business and employees will be the hatching of new delivery or acquisition systems. A nearly 30-year-old medical example should suggest future dental possibilities. A pioneer, Kaiser Industries, has long said that its extensive medical services for employees are supplied at far lower costs than comparable services obtained in the usual ways.

A more recent example is the delivery of medical services to residents of the "new city" of Columbia, Maryland. The influence of the coming supercorporations on the huge movement toward new cities will be treated in Part Three of this book. For our immediate purpose of diagnosing the dynamic effects of supers on all kinds of services, let us simply note that in this new city, the cost of a doctor's visit is only $2.00. This is an element of the city's commercial plan to provide comprehensive health care, balanced between prevention and treatment.

The overall venture in Columbia is also commercially sponsored by Connecticut General Life Insurance Co. Thus, we say that supercorporations and semisupers will make fundamental changes in many services, of which dental care is only one previously unexpected example. These changes, even when they increase the demand for services, will in most cases lead to better values for postindustrial corporations and their employees. The better values will not come easily, but will be shaped by a combination of frontal corporate pounding and of corporate fathering of new acquisition and delivery systems for services.

Trade associations. Although there are a number of treasured exceptions, trade associations have been less than leaders in the American business community. Some have been lairs for price fixing.

Some other trade associations have been more oriented toward socializing and entertainment. Too many have been performing routine jobs in a routine way for routine membership dues. A few insiders among the memberships have worked hard, and some have had the satisfaction of moving up the hierarchies to become top officials in their industry groups. In some cases, the politics and the climbing have been more consuming activities than the providing of services to members.

Also, some associations drag along near the stalling speed, sputtering to stay aloft on small and sometimes red-ink budgets. Of these, a fortunate group still has liquid reserves left over from a more relaxed day.

All this is too familiar to most business people to require more than this notation of both the excellent trade associations and a number of run-down hangers-on.

In contrast, supercorporations, as imperfect as they must be as a human institution, will be moving more directly than the average corporation toward improving levels of efficiency.

In their interface with the trade associations, the supers and their emulators will be dealing with an industry composed of over 35,000 organizations of all types, with aggregate income in the hundreds of millions of dollars. Two earmarks of supercorporations will help to leave trade associations not quite the same any more: greater internal incentives for the supers' own employees, and, again, flexibility.

Greater opportunities, with the associated greater incentives, that will have to enliven the supers will cause a larger share of their people to use their time better, and will thus bear on whatever the better supercorporation people do and don't do. Individual executives and employees themselves will have to do some weeding out of unprofitable activity. Some of them will decide to reduce their personal activity in their trade associations, to attend meetings less often, or simply to cancel their membership.

Flexibility is the second characteristic of supercorporations that will do in some of the trade associations' former support. At the simplest level, the harder-nosed managers in supers will be less reluctant to sever old ties, if the only reason for keeping those ties is their advanced age. The thought that anything that has been done the same way for 20 years must be wrong will figure in some no-go decisions on trade association memberships and activities. What people think of supers' profits and growth will be progressively more important to their managers than what people think of their pulling out of some heirloom trade association relationships.

To be sure, trade associations will reap some gains from this same super flexibility. Some of the corporate loners who stayed out at some cost to themselves ought to be found doing some reevaluating. The net effect of flexibility could be either a down or an up for trade associations as a category.

In another aspect of flexibility, supers are far more likely to question the fixed assumptions underlying the existence of trade associations. These organizations may not be the most productive in governmental relations for all industries and circumstances. For example, it was a commonplace in Washington, D.C., to say that if a particular medical organization was against a bill, then the Congress would surely pass it.

In addition, trade associations may or may not be cost effective av-

enues for published communications in an industry. Some associations' publications are among the front-runners, even against well-
financed profit-making competition. Others will not stand the scrutiny
of someone flexible enough to take a good look.

Without running through the catalog of association activities, some
flexible supercorporation members will shake up these activities before
they fail to renew their memberships. Other representatives of supers
will rock the boat even more by their insistence on new, flexible activities, while choosing to remain as less shepherded members.

The supercorporations' more incisive evaluations and actions probably will have two broader effects on their trade association relationships: a kind of political multiplier phenomenon and an increase in
consolidations and deaths.

First, the political multiplier effect. Start with the usually unmen-
tioned fact that we businessmen too often are a community of sheep
when it comes to trade association matters. In a typical situation, a
showdown demonstrated that only about 50 older men were making all
the decisions, political and otherwise, for a 60-year-old national association of over 1,200 members. (This was one of the money-losers that
was feeding off its remaining cash reserves.) Just a few sure and clear
voices could have turned that association around in a matter of weeks,
but those voices were never raised. The same is true of thousands of
other trade associations, local and regional as well as national.

Now, when the supers begin to cut down or phase out some of
their inherited trade association memberships and activities, they will
normally have some coldly logical findings and reasons. Even if partly
kept quiet or stated graciously, these negative findings and conclusions
will in some cases start more of us sheep calling for a new direction,
one that will say "perform or perish" to many association activities
and to some associations themselves. Thus the newly heard voices of a
few may be multiplied by the acceptance of many other members,
nonsupers included.

Second, the obituary columns. With members and prospective
members demanding more of associations, some will not make it. The
two leading choices, to combine or die, will have to be made more
frequently in the later 1970s and the 1980s.

This is intended, not as a ghoulish conclusion, but as a vibrant
one. The pallid clinging together in obsolete or senile organizations
will be replaced, to a degree, by the application of some more busi-

nesslike practices to associations of businessmen. The supercorporation will be in the van, and the surviving trade associations will be the finer for it.

Trade publications. With respect to this industry of over 2,300 publications and annual sales approaching a billion dollars, two possible effects of supers bear watching. One is the chance that supers will enter the trade press field by acquiring strings of profitable and fast-growing publications; the other is that supers will start up some of their own trade publishing operations. In earnings, most trade publishers are small potatoes relative to large corporations and will be even smaller relative to the burgeoning supercorporations. The supers will be able to bridge the size gap by either of these two means.

As difficult as it is to earn large, growing, and dependable profits, a few publishing entrepreneurs and managers have this ability. Either as a sheer diversification or as a profit center operationally related to others, certain acquisition opportunities can be useful for a limited number of supercorporations that are interested in the trade publications field. The mere fact that most nonpublishing corporations have instinctively stayed out of the industry has left a population base suitable for supers to assemble a few good profit centers. But this kind— or any kind—of publishing is sufficiently specialized that a supercorporation probably will enter the field only if it already has a proved entrepreneur or manager from within the industry.

One can hear a clamor about conflicts of interest between a trade publication and its extremely profit-minded owner, a supercorporation that is mostly not a publishing enterprise. Yes, there could be conflicts of interest, more easily than not. There may be no way for a super to avoid them and still get into publishing. In this event, the solution is likely to be disclosure of the conflict, rather than foreclosure of the opportunity.

The second route by which a few supers might move into trade and business-periodical publishing is the expedient of trying to make a profit center out of what is usually a cost center. We have recognized the more intense profit orientation of supercorporations. This applies to small matters as well as large ones. At this early date, more and more conventional corporations are selling the services of departments that used to be considered as inevitable overhead. This same rationale is likely to be applied to publishing. Taking a step directly into a form of publishing, General Electric has advertised its economic forecasting service to all comers for $450 per year. Whether this nonpublisher's move into publishing means an expansion of the market or a tightening of competition, or both, the trailblazing for supercorporations in publishing has already been started.

The smallness of the profit that a company like GE makes on a publishing venture grown out of an overhead department is not the measure to be used. Anyone experienced in running a large business knows that a profit has to be squeezed out of every likely and unlikely corner, sometimes by the penny. Of equal importance is the tone that is set by action, not words. When the office of the chairman shows that it is interested in the small amounts to be made from a kind of publishing venture, then it is also getting through more effectively to the switchgear, aerospace, and hundreds of other profit and cost centers that every penny of profit had better be produced there, too. This also cuts the ground out from under those line managers whose too relaxed attitude toward overhead costs is endlessly explained away by their pointing to all kinds of "unnecessary" overhead in the corporate headquarters. So some supercorporations, on the basis of the experience of a few large conventional corporations, are likely to enter the trade press field by the expedient of trying to turn a publishing-related overhead department into a profit center.

One smaller possibility exists: the venture-management groups of supercorporations may advance the capital for the founding or expansion of some publishers' ventures. American Express put up some of the venture capital for a new general circulation newsmagazine, and others could find it similarly interesting to back a new trade publication. As in the expected publishing efforts by supers themselves, such venture financing will be incidental to the mainstream of the supers' growth. However, for the publishers thus financed, the supers' participation will be not incidental but vital.

The change to a service-based economy. The often repeated story of the U.S. economy's switch from a products base to a base increasingly centered on services has been heralded by some as another advance in our standard of living. There have been other, less happy thoughts about a service economy. One, all too close to everyone's home, is that services cannot be run as capably and purveyed as efficiently as most manufacturing. Airplanes, for instance, as products, fly quite well, but airline services do not measure up to the quality and reliability of the airplanes themselves.

Second, and more crucial to the growth of the economy, services are harder to automate or rationalize. It is more difficult to increase productivity in the immature service groups than to raise factory and warehouse productivity. The arbitrator hearing a labor dispute and the hospital orderly emptying a bedpan cannot be speeded up as was the auto production worker when he was moved from the workbench to an assembly line.

There may be little theoretical weakness in these and other ideas about the inherent inefficiency and susceptibility to inflation of a U.S. economy based increasingly on services. There is another side to the story, the pragmatic business and human side—in what I call the microfuture. In this form of forecasting, we consider especially the role of corporations as a "small" part of postindustrial society. In this frame of reference, supercorporations and their emulators will be unexpectedly powerful movers and shakers.

All services can become more productive. For example, the fixed minimum attorney's fees in the purchase and sale of property, which until recently have somehow escaped the attention of antitrust lawyers, are likely to go down, and without impairing the quality or delivery of essential services. If a service cannot be automated, its cost can be reduced by more than 50 percent—and how many automation projects take 50 percent out of product costs? Similarly, consulting fees of $400 per day and more paid to young people who would earn more like $100 to $150 per day if they were on the client's own payroll are not likely to continue to grow apace in the next 15 years. There is no more wrong with those bright, peppy young people than there is with the lawyers who serve their clients in real estate transactions. Nor, again, is there anything wrong at the theoretical level with the concept of inevitable inefficiency in services. The only thing that is wrong—and supers are going to change this—is that natural competitive pressure has been weak or nonexistent.

Hence, we may conclude that the theory of the inevitable inefficiency of services is overblown, and that the apparently unrelated coming of the new supercorporations is going to trigger some monumental changes in the service groups, as well as similar but lesser changes in the manufacturing sector of our economy. Efforts will be made to keep the services as comfortable and as profitable as they have been. Legislative defenses will be set up and later knocked down. More codes of ethics will be composed, with subsequent decomposition. There will be stormy meetings with customers and clients, dire predictions of the messes that will pile up through changes in service arrangements, and not a few ruptured friendships and associations. But after all the predictable wailing and gnashing of teeth, there will really be a far more efficient, effective complex of services in the U.S. economy. Theoretically impossible, perhaps, but actually on the way.

Multiple Captives

Supercorporations will take the lead in bringing about yet another pervasive change in the marketplace, and again competition as we know it will never be the same. This change will involve setting up many more joint or cooperative enterprises to serve two or more captive customers. I have coined the name "multiple captives" for these enterprises. The captive ventures will remind you partly of standard joint ventures and partly of the cooperative movement in the United States.

Most of us have known of one or two multiple captives, but they still require a little describing. Some of the present multiple captives are the clearing houses, or clearing corporations, owned and run by the larger banks in major metropolitan areas; the nonprofit Associated Press, owned by over 4,900 newspapers and radio and television stations, which provides a range of news-gathering and other services that few if any of its sponsors could provide as well for themselves; and the data processing service organizations set up by regional groups of Catholic hospitals. There are more, but only a handful, compared to the numbers of multiple captives that will be established with the rise of supercorporations, semisupers, and their many emulators.

If you want to forget, in daily usage, the special nature of the multiple captives and just call them joint ventures, that's fine. But some will find it useful to know the following differences between a typical joint venture and that other entity I call a multiple captive.

Starting on familiar ground, the typical joint venture is a profit-making entity, usually set up to deal with the markets, supplies, or technologies among the venturing corporations. It is usually fathered by two parent corporations that often have equal shares in the ownership of the venture. Some joint ventures are later bought up by one of the original partners, with or without an original plan to do so.

Now come the differences. Most important, the purpose of the multiple captive is to take over and operate overhead or staff functions in order to reduce greatly their cost and burden. It is usually set up by three or more founding companies, which may or may not own equal shares. And it is likely to continue permanently, because the underlying need for the multiple captive is unlikely to change so much as to cause its abandonment. Furthermore, the multiple captive may be a profit-making or nonprofit business.

Thus, the differences between joint ventures and multiple captives begin to come into focus. The profit-making joint venture can capture a profit opportunity by drawing on the several capabilities of its parent companies, as in the case of Dow Corning Corp. The profit or nonprofit multiple captive is set up by quite a number of sponsoring organizations to take some kind of common function or administrative headache from the sponsors and put it into a separate entity. The joint venture usually provides its owners with a new profit-making opportunity that might not otherwise exist, whereas the multiple captive begins by dealing with functions that must exist, whether or not the multiple captive is formed to handle them. To put it all together, the joint venture is created to operate a potentially profit-making new enterprise, whereas the multiple captive inherits from its sponsors some of the necessary operating and housekeeping functions that are uneconomical, unwanted, or impossible for the individual companies to handle on their own.

There now seems to be a distinction with a difference. The distinctiveness of the multiple captive is its lackluster quality. It does not capture the emotions as does the glamorous growth company. It may not even be profitable, but may only reduce the costs or losses that would have accrued without it.

Climbing out on a limb again, I expect that scores or hundreds of new multiple captives will cut costs of overhead departments for their sponsors in many ways. For example, there will probably be more computer service centers and facilities management centers owned by and operated for groups of similar companies. Multiple captives may somehow be set up in trucking, the International Brotherhood of Teamsters and the ICC notwithstanding. Other multiple captives could replace many corporations' travel departments and still others could eliminate much of the uneconomical and competitive printing of newspapers.

Just since these pages were originally drafted there has been a noticeable increase in multiple captives—as predicted. A group of freight shippers in central Iowa, including a fertilizer manufacturer and a lumber dealer, bought a branch railroad line abandoned by the Chicago Rock Island and Pacific Railroad. After nine months of no rail service, the shipper-owners again have the rail service they consider vital. Perhaps a few dozen more such multiple captive rail operations will be formed, with shipper groups in New York State alone trying to form six of them.

Also, Knight Newspapers, Inc., and Tribune Company formed a supplemental news service to assemble and market up to 250 stories and specialty columns per week from the newspapers owned by these two sponsors, plus a third newspaper, *The National Observer*. In addition, five major companies have pledged $500,000 each to start a $7.5 million research and development program for the recovery of oil from shale. The original sponsors are Standard Oil Co. (Ohio), Gulf Oil Corp., Cleveland-Cliffs Iron Co., Southern California Edison Co., and Arthur G. McKee & Co. These companies hope for at least 10 other sponsors for this multiple captive.

And there is a new European multiple captive, formed by four daily newspapers which plan to publish a monthly multinational business newspaper called *Europa*. It will be distributed as a supplement to the sponsoring newspapers' 5.5 million readers.

As regards the entire economy, the use of multiple captives in scores of additional applications and industries will lead to net increments in overall efficiency. The negative general effect, which seems less important, is the reduction in the number of competitors that will occur when each new multiple captive amalgamates the formerly separate activities that had been lodged in each of the several to a dozen or more sponsoring companies.

For individuals and companies, the good effect of more multiple captives will include the greater opportunities created by the existence of these far more efficient entities. On the minus side will be numbers of business and personal dislocations. These will hit first within the departments or divisions cut down, phased out, or transferred to each new multiple captive. The second negative effect will be the personal and business losses caused in supplier companies by lost and changed customers and by the smaller requirements for products and services on the part of the new multiple captives. These simply will need less of everything to do the same job more efficiently than their many separate predecessors.

Now let us review the overall effects of supercorporations on competition in the U.S. business economy. First, supers will engage in less than their share of destructive price-cutting competition and more than their share of competition in new product and new service development and improvement. This would strengthen U.S. business competition, except in the arena of nose-bloodying price cuts on the same old standard commodities and services.

Although some smaller companies dealing with supercorporations as customers or suppliers will be hurt by the supers' more rational and demanding policies, others will be helped by more enlightened procurement policies. The net effect may be damage to the weaker of the smaller companies and benefit to the better managed smaller companies. In any event, increasing antitrust litigation, plus the supers' own growth demands on themselves, will tend to make the business world of the supercorporations more competitive, rather than less so.

One of the important aspects of supercorporate influence on competition concerns the sometimes unimaginative area of make-versus-buy decisions. Among the predictable results will be a net increase in the "make" decisions over the "buy" decisions, especially in services; far more stringent requirements for the performance and cost effectiveness of those products and services that will still be bought; some elimination of services and products formerly deemed essential; some acquisitions and some launchings of service groups as new profit centers for supers; and some venture-capital investments by supers in both product and service fields.

All suppliers to large corporations will thus be greatly changed, but the service group will be hit harder than the manufacturers of products. Focusing on representative services, I foresee a possibility that supercorporations will exert pressure against increases in fee levels for professionals such as dentists, as well as a chance that supers will take the lead in developing more efficient acquisition and delivery systems for professional services.

Supercorporations will have a small direct impact, and larger ultimate consequences, on trade associations, because of both the improving effectiveness of some of the supers' own employees and the application of their corporate flexibility. The results will be a few more individual supercorporation memberships, but also a net decline in super membership in trade associations. Also, there will be some combination of decline and death among the associations themselves.

Supers can have far-reaching effects on specific trade publishers and still greater influences on that industry as a whole. In addition to being bigger users of editorial content and tougher buyers of advertising, some supercorporations may acquire series of periodicals and set up the resulting publishing enterprises within their own structure. Others may start new publications as a means of turning a former overhead cost center into a small but useful profit center, or may support publishing enterprises as multiple captives. Still others may provide venture financing to a few publishers for starting or expanding trade and business publishing enterprises.

For the entire service group, I predict much more cost effective arrangements throughout the postindustrial business community in the United States, the theory that services are inherently inefficient notwithstanding.

Tougher and smarter make-versus-buy decisions on the part of supercorporations and semisupers, with others following suit, will lead to an increase of several hundred percent in the number of multiple captive corporations—some profit-oriented and others going the nonprofit route—in the 1970s and 1980s. These additional multiple captives, set up by two or more corporate sponsors in order to handle more efficiently some functions that the sponsors would otherwise have to continue to handle less efficiently for themselves, will invade fields where they have been little used to date, causing some personal disasters for displaced employees and corporations.

On balance, however, the spectacular expansion of the number and scope of these multiple captive companies will result in net benefits to the business community and to the economy because of their considerable increases in productivity and general economic efficiency. Supercorporations will support this movement doubly, by making more than proportional use of existing and new multiple captives, and by showing the way for other large companies.

In the world of supercorporations, then, some competitors will gain, while others will lose or fail. Competition, which does really exist in the United States, will be more seriously practiced by more companies, under the goad of the supercorporations' hunger for record growth.

7

CHANGES in CORPORATE LIFE and STRUCTURE

SUPERCORPORATIONS will bring about surpassing changes in corporate life, especially for leaders and managers, from directors and chief executive officers down to foremen and subdepartment supervisors. Regrettably, the most remarkable changes may not yet be foreseeable. But those that can be guessed at are many, and these will penetrate every pore of corporate life. Before we proceed to a discussion of these changes, a basic assumption of this book needs to be examined.

I have predicated much of the business landscape of the later 1970s and the 1980s on the basis of that of the early 1970s. Before this placid assumption is further used, it should be bounced against a group of earlier and far more startling projections by other futurists. These are the models of a U.S. society in which few people are required to work very much, and these few support all the others at good and rising standards of living. If this should actually happen by 1990, then the more workaday projections of Part Two could not occur.

Nearly a quarter-century ago a group of futurists began predicting great change from the situation in which work is necessary to support life. In 1954, Norbert Wiener, of the Massachusetts Institute of Technology, said, in *The Human Use of Human Beings,* "It is perfectly clear that this [the "automatic machine"] will produce an unemployment situation, in comparison with which . . . even the depression of the thirties will seem a pleasant joke." [1] That is the depression which, in the United States, saw 12.8 million workers, 25 percent of the workforce, unemployed.

By 1962, Donald Michael not only affirmed the Wiener thesis, but also prophesied that dire family consequences would follow the largely leisure-filled life of the former and nominal breadwinner. Mr. Michael thought, for example, that the father would be working fewer hours than his children would be required to spend in school and on homework, with attendant family tensions. [2]

Further, in 1963, Dennis Gabor, of the University of London, became convinced that "For the first time in history we are now faced with the possibility of a world in which only a minority need work, to keep the great majority in idle luxury." [3] This extraordinary shift, from more than 90 percent of the workforce employed to well under 25 percent employed, would require a new ethic: ". . . if we want to achieve such a [better] world, we shall need much intelligence, but even more charity. The leading minority must forget that the 'majority' are objectively useless because they could be replaced by machines." [4]

Well, in this light, does one shut off his concern for today's business world and brood about the attitude of the "leading minority" toward the "objectively useless" majority? No, not yet. Instead, I make the flat assumption that these prophecies will not come to pass in our time frame of the remainder of the 1970s and the 1980s. There now appears to be far too much work to be done, especially the kind that is not to be done by Wiener's "automatic machine." The human-based service economy, which the United States has already entered, has to be more than 16 years away from displacement by automated devices for handling educational, medical, rehabilitation, leisure, and other services. Also, the amounts and intensity of the work required to rebuild cities, help develop the Third World, solve the energy crisis, clean up the environment, and perform other nonautomatable tasks must engage 90 percent or more of the U.S. population at least until 1990.

[1] New York: Avon, 1954, p. 189.
[2] *Cybernation—The Silent Conquest* (Santa Barbara, Calif.: Center for the Study of Democratic Institutions, 1962), p. 31.
[3] *Inventing the Future* (New York: Knopf, 1964), p. 133.
[4] Ibid., p. 140.

Choose among your futurists. If you conclude, contrary to this book, that a small proportion of the U.S. population is all that will be needed to operate and grow an annual economy of more than \$2.75 trillion within the next 15 years or so, then the significance of the supercorporation is nil. But if you agree with me that the largely automatic economy, if it comes at all, will not arrive before the twenty-first century, then the more immediate coming of the supercorporations and semisupers should concern you.

One point that everyone should agree on is that the supers will not come automatically and without effort. They will be hewn and pounded out of groaning conventional corporations by bands of determined men doing a lot of things differently. What specific kinds of change will both cause and result from the emergence of supercorporations? On the basis of changes in some large conventional corporations in recent years, we can project some of the things that will happen in corporate management. As with the other effects of supers we have discussed, there is likely to be some carry-over of management changes into semisupers and many other companies in the United States.

The next three chapters discuss three aspects of corporate living: the wider use of the growth function we now call venture management; a supercorporation attempt at managing people; and the broader use of manpower planning as a powerful tool instead of a mere fad. This chapter deals in detail with a fourth area, modifications in organizational structure at the highest levels, and then goes on to review some aspects of the supercorporations' general invasion of corporate life.

Top-Level Change: The Office of the Chairman

It is unusual, even in America, to organize and manage a corporation of billion-dollar size. It is far more unusual to contemplate a giant of this size that is to grow twice as fast as smaller companies. Only a few extraordinary managements can pull it off, and one of their first tasks is to get themselves organized structurally. Just as a supercorporation is to be a different kind of corporation, and not simply an oversized conventional corporation, so also the super's top management setup may have to be different in kind from most of the structures used to date by less aggressive enterprises.

One simple example gives the flavor of organizational complexity. As a business grows, the network of its organizational relationships increases at a much faster rate than the number of its executives. The little business that has one boss and only three supervisors immediately below him has only six possible relationships with which to deal. If this little organization doubles in size and adds three more supervisors, it does not have twice the six relationships of the original structure; it now has 21 relationships. Extend this formula to the corporations employing 10,000 to 100,000 people and you begin to sketch in the problems of organizing a structure that will somehow permit the business to function.

Any solution to these problems principally involves the perhaps 100,000 to 150,000 top- and upper-level executives of large corporations in the United States, plus the several hundred thousand others who are out to get their bosses' jobs. The solutions have never been clear, and more often than not they have ended up as exasperating patch jobs. As an added complication, the supercorporation will be not just a bigger centipede but one that is much faster and lighter on its feet than the familiar corporate giant. Now, how does one organize for both greater size and greater agility even before the older top management organizational problems have been very well solved? Is any solution at all in sight? Yes, one seems to be. It is the idea variously known as the office of the chief executive, or the office of the president, or the corporate office. I call the concept the office of the chairman.

The concept involves the organization of a number of executives, usually from two to six, into a single chief executive group to handle the duties formerly discharged just by the chairman or the president or both. After we get past the immediate objection that you can't have two (or six) bosses, we can see that the concept has validity.

Here, again, as in nearly all the cases in this book, it is necessary to use the actions of present-day corporations in an attempt to illustrate the supercorporation of the future. Much of the data is from a study I directed of the experiences of 17 major U.S. corporations with the office of the chairman.

It will be surprising to many executives to find that at least 30 to 40 large U.S. corporations have used, or are using, the office of the chairman as their preferred means of organizing at the top. The users have included Armstrong Cork, Bell & Howell, Bendix, Caterpillar Tractor, General Electric, IBM, R. H. Macy, Manufacturers Hanover

Trust, McGraw-Hill, National Biscuit, Singer, TRW, and the Times Mirror Company. This still relatively unknown and unrecognized form of top management organization has been in effect in individual companies for periods up to seven years, to date. Many companies have found the office of the chairman to be more than an experiment or an expedient.

THE OFFICE OF THE CHAIRMAN—A DESCRIPTION

The most common, and partially overlapping, reasons for adopting the office of the chairman are to provide more total time for top executives, to enable top executives to devote more time to external affairs, to foster and facilitate strategic or long-range planning, and, sometimes, to provide a mix of backgrounds in a diversified company.

These reasons for adopting the office of the chairman tie directly to the difficulties and frustrations familiar to anyone who has been involved with top management. For instance, it is often extremely difficult to get decisions made, even when the chief executive officer and his assistants are working 10 to 14 hours a day. Furthermore, large corporations entail almost unthinkable complexities, which are being further compounded by additional socioeconomic considerations. The problems of communication and executive participation in large corporations have been widely publicized and often studied. There are the risky questions of top management succession and the underrecognized hangups of integrating major mergers and acquisitions.

Some creative basis must be found for imposing order and extricating top management from this morass. One solution is the office of the chairman. When this new office is first created, from one to four senior executives are usually removed from their previous line or staff positions and placed into it, joining the chairman and/or the president. Then other executives are promoted to replace the newly elevated senior executives. The next step is to free the two- to six-man office of the chairman of divisional, department, and routine staff duties, thus enabling it to devote all its time to the top management functions of planning, organizing, directing, and controlling the business and handling external relations.

The executives who formerly reported to the chairman or president personally now report to the office of the chairman as an entity. Plans and decisions that formerly were channeled only to the chairman and the president (and their assistants) now can be acted on by one to four more top men, each of whom is formally authorized to act for the office of the chairman. Within individual limits, each member of the office is free to make a decision that binds the entire corporation.

A chief executive surrounded by assistants awaiting his decisions is clearly different from a group of two to six executives who *make* decisions, rather than wait for them. The following list highlights the principal differences between a corporate structure using the office of the chairman and a typical top management organizational structure with its usual line and staff elements.

Characteristic	Chairman/President Structure	Office of the Chairman
Number of top decision makers	Two, the chairman and the president.	From two to six or more, usually at least four.
Range of talents and experience of top decision makers	Restricted to ranges of the chairman and the president.	Several times greater.
Reporting relationships of top subordinates	Report to the chairman or the president.	Report to the office of the chairman.
Clarity of reporting relationships	Entirely clear and simple. This most familiar form of relationships may seem clearer to those accustomed to it.	As clear and simple as in traditional structures, but is less familiar to participants.
Who makes top management decisions?	Usually only the chairman or the president is authorized to make top management decisions.	Usually any one of the two to six members is authorized to make decisions on his own, if necessary.
Length of decision time	Impossible to generalize, but some large corporations find that top management decisions take months.	Impossible to generalize, but two to three times as many top decision makers can cut decision time by more than half, without loss of quality.

An example will illustrate the potent workings of this still unfamiliar method of organizing the large corporation at the top: A leading U.S. commercial bank (not Manufacturers Hanover, cited above) has been using successfully the office-of-the-chairman structure for five years. One instance of its effectiveness will indicate the general advantages of this structure. Like other major banks, this one was expanding rapidly overseas. The head of its foreign operations had found that it was taking too long to get top management decisions on crucial matters. Since the adoption of the office-of-the-chairman structure, the decision time has been reduced by more than half, and top bank officers believe that better decisions are being made. As a result, the office of the chairman is considered by these officers to be the right top management structure.

An acid test of the office of the chairman is the evaluation by those who have used it and subsequently terminated it. The former users have changed to other organizational forms because of changes in their businesses or their top people, not because of structural flaws in the concept.

For instance, Federated Department Stores announced in 1973 that it was replacing its four-man executive office by a two-man management team consisting of the chairman and the president. The executive office was in effect in Federated for only about seven months, and its termination came with the appointment of a new president. According to the official announcement, the new arrangement "formalizes a partnership between us [the chairman and the new president] that has developed during the past year and a half since he became vice-chairman." Federated also said that the two current top executives had given themselves five years to "identify and qualify" their successors. This company's experiment with, and abandonment of, its version of the office of the chairman was thus closely tied to major shifts in top executives.

Similarly, one of the largest chemicals companies terminated its office of the chairman when the participants changed; the new chief executive officer did not wish to continue this structure with a new and different membership.

If the office of the chairman is being used successfully in some large conventional corporations, wherein might it relate to supercorporations?

THE OFFICE OF THE CHAIRMAN AND THE SUPERCORPORATION

This brief treatment of the office of the chairman leaves most of the subject to others, but it gives some guideposts to the changes in top corporate organization that may come with the emergence of supercorporations. The supers will have a magnified set of the top organizational problems mentioned earlier. Because they will be more diversified than most conventional corporations, more intense stress will be put on the personal range of their top executives. Because they will be both large and conspicuous, and perhaps controversial as well, the outside demands on their top corporate officers will exceed those made on most conventional corporate officers. With more rapid growth, aggressiveness, flexibility, and creativity at the heart, they will be subject to communication problems that can barely be imagined. Thus they will have an extreme need for effective organization at the top. Although the office-of-the-chairman structure is but one alternative, it is a time-giving alternative to those whose corporate lives are plagued by a perpetual lack of time.

I predict that the supercorporations will account for more than their share of use of the office of the chairman. In addition, remember the fad syndrome. Some business executives copy one another's actions. Most of the thousands of conventional corporations will probably never use multiple management at the top level. But the number of users will increase by dozens or scores, some of them merely following the fashion set by the supers.

EFFECTS ON INDIVIDUAL EXECUTIVES

The adoption of the office-of-the-chairman structure will bring about a series of changes in the corporate life of individual executives. These changes will be mostly worthwhile, but will produce some innocent and guilty victims in and around the executive suite. The specific changes will be many, quiet, and cumulative.

The sheer necessity of making good decisions much faster will change the tempo of the corporate lives of most managers and supervisors, up and down the line. When major decisions are reached in weeks instead of months, the reaction time of all managers outside the office of the chairman will have to speed up. Thus, in an age in which we have not yet learned to keep up with the present rate of change, a more rapid rate of change in the supers and other large corporations is already pressing upon us. The creation of an office of the chairman can be expected to set off a series of jostlings and fittings within a corporation—though not so obviously and not so soon as with a total reorganization. Those who can march to a faster pace will move in and up, and vice versa.

Another difference in corporate life-style will be a hard-nosed demand for better decisions, recommendations, and plans from managers outside the office of the chairman. In today's large conventional corporations, decisions are still sometimes made by catching the boss at his desk for a quick telephone conversation or on his way to the company jet. But when the number of top decision makers is augmented 100 to 300 percent, subordinates' shots from the hip will be less acceptable. The cronies, the personality men, the politicians and political legatees, the overpromoted, the obsolete—all these will remain in and around top management, but their mortality will increase notably. The Peter Principle will get more attention. The talents of most of those who rise to the office of the chairman will have been adequate to screen out much of the shoddy work by subordinates, and there will now be two or three times as much opportunity to evaluate such inputs. The quality of the inputs will increase, and the population of those providing poor inputs will shrink—not overnight, but through time.

From the immediate objection to having six bosses to the quiet conviction of those who have successfully used the office of the chairman is a long span. The conceptual and practical difficulties of this structure can be handled in a treatise, but the satisfaction and the assurance in the eyes and voices of these top executives probably must be felt in person. The office of the chairman as a form of top corporate organization will be sometimes misunderstood and often controversial, but it will remain and flower.

The office of the chairman will contribute to the formation of some supers by adding to the effectiveness of their top managements. In other companies, this structure will follow the arrival of super status, because it will be adopted to ease the excruciating crunch at the top of those fast-moving giants.

To review, the office of the chairman is one unfamiliar organizational structure that will be used by a number of the coming supercorporations. Taking various names, this structure will add from one to four or five decision makers to top management. Better and faster decisions will be made, and the extreme performance standards of the supers will thereby more likely be met.

The office of the chairman, when adopted as the top management organizational structure by both supers and more conventional corporations, must lead to a different life for executives. Two differences that will affect managers will be the need for faster response time and the demand for better plans, recommendations, and decisions. Some managers will rise to these and other needs and will prosper. Others will not, and the organizational structure of the office of the chairman may lead directly to their downfall.

The use of this newer organizational structure by supercorporations, with its repercussions for executives and for other corporations, is but one of at least five major changes in the U.S. business environment that will probably result from the evolution of supercorporations. Before we go on to the innovation of venture management, let us look briefly at some of the other ways in which the supercorporate invasion of corporate life will be felt.

The Supercorporate Invasion of Corporate Life

What about all the paraphernalia of marketing, budgeting, and the other conventional corporate functions? The supercorporations, semi-supers, and their emulators will no doubt provide a new, rigorous environment for all of these. This section offers some condensed observations.

Corporate Planning

Corporate planning is the function that will probably be most affected by supercorporations, and that, in turn, will be of milestone importance to them. Few, if any, conventional corporations or swinging conglomerates can step up to super status without different and better corporate planning than they have had. In addition, as the supers develop, not only will they be using corporate planning with a rare capability, they will be refining and improving the entire corporate-planning process.

Actually, this whole volume is about corporate planning. But it is not a manual of corporate planning; rather it is a hunting license for those interested in corporate planning for supers or for corporations competing with supers.

THE SYSTEMS APPROACH

Here, too, supercorporations will make major contributions and profit greatly by innovations. General Electric's extensive systems study of, and program for working with, disadvantaged employees is a model of the application of systems logic and power to corporate areas previously untouched by the systems approach.

Categorically, the systems approach to defining and solving intricate problems in mammoth companies will be a major determinant of the supercorporations' achievements. Also, their leadership in practical systems approaches will create interest and spread expertise in ever widening systems approaches in many other corporations.

COMPUTERIZED INFORMATION SYSTEMS AND DATA PROCESSING

This field is still one of the fastest growing of our era. Some inventors believe that we have seen only the smallest part of the benefits and effects to come from computerized information systems and data processing.

In addition to the supercorporations' use of computers in manpower planning, which is discussed in Chapter 10, the supers will be among the biggest users of computerized information systems and data processing—proportionally, as well as in terms of their annual costs. The stepping up of corporate planning alone will raise the supers' patronage of this whole field. The systems approach, while not restricted to computer support, will use increasing amounts of computer time. The rapidity of super growth will make computers and systems more essential and economical for supercorporations than for companies with plenty of time to absorb fewer changes.

The cost-effectiveness upbringing of supercorporation people should not be overlooked. Increases in the sophistication of computer and systems usage will give some hard knocks to hardware, software, and service vendors, as well as to the supers' own computer and systems people. In a few cases, to achieve greater cost effectiveness, computers will be thrown out. Some of these casualties will be replaced with minicomputers, with outside time sharing, or in other ways. Other computers and systems, even in the late 1970s and 1980s, will be retired in favor of manual or mechanical replacements. A big shake-out is coming, and the supers will be among the breakaway merchants of change.

Lastly, the human factor will be of the greatest importance in the relationship between supercorporations and computers. The somewhat smarter, more impatient breed of new managers who will run the supers will be computer oriented. They will be at home with computers and will want to use them far more thoroughly than is typical today. These hard-driving supermanagers will have their own way, taking giant steps with the advanced computers and systems.

MARKETING AND THE MARKETING CONCEPT

The marketing function will be another of the chief beneficiaries of the advent of supercorporations. The corporate entrepreneurship that will be *the* distinguishing mark of the super will put an emphasis on marketing—not just on peddling or salesmanship—that has been missing in many conventional corporations. Marketing, and the marketing concept, are close to the essence of starting successful new businesses. Some of the supers will be properly lauded in future trade paper stories as great marketers.

This special attention to marketing should also have an effect on who gets the top jobs in supercorporations. It will be the corporate entrepreneurs who rise to the top in the supers, and the marketing people are naturally better positioned than most to move up. We will still get lawyers, financial experts, production experts, and others as top executives in the supers, but with a critical difference. In the past, some large corporations put lawyers and other specialists into top spots *because* they were lawyers, or schooled in some other needed specialty, such as finance or manufacturing. No more. In supers, women and men with these and other specialized backgrounds will more often rise to the top because they have become outstanding corporate entrepreneurs, not because they are good specialists.

INVESTMENT AND COMMERCIAL BANKING

I have frequently counseled chief executive officers to strengthen these all-important relationships. While most supercorporations will automatically do so, they will also take up some restructuring of services, fees, and relationships.

Both commercial banking and investment banking have been tentatively moving toward more specific service policies, direct fees for work done, and more businesslike, less clubby relationships. This is right in line with the supers' rational approach to business effectiveness. As with any intensely rational process, some of the warmth and comfort of time-honored relationships will inevitably be shouldered out. Nevertheless, supers will respond to the trends that commercial and investment bankers have already initiated and will start or force others. They will even take over some of the functions of these financial institutions and do them in-house. Shades of make-versus-buy again.

BOARDS OF DIRECTORS

We have finally begun to realize that too many boards of directors of major corporations have been functioning more as moribund gentlemen's clubs than as ultimate governing bodies. I predict that many influences will shake up the institution of the board of directors. There will be more stockholder derivative suits, more attacks by environmentalists and minority groups, and possibly some direct actions by governments. Added to all this will be the competitive and other pressures that the supercorporations will exert on many other companies.

As a consequence, these boards, numbering in the tens of thousands, will be meeting oftener, staying longer, doing more homework, and getting more unscheduled phone calls from the chief executive officer. A number of them will wind up voting themselves out of office by approving the sale or merger of their companies with a supercorporation. In other cases, the sale or merger will be to a nonsuper company, but will have been triggered by the good or bad influence of one or more supers. In the supers themselves, the boards will become what they were intended to be—the ultimate authority.

GOVERNMENT EMPLOYEES

Perhaps someone else will write at length about the influences of supercorporations on government employees. We will see some of these effects in later discussions of supers in public-private partnerships and in the contract state. These super shocks will be very hard on tens of thousands of government employees.

One remotely possible effect that we can mention at this point relates especially to government employees at the upper levels. It may be that the combination of the greater effectiveness of supers, their much higher and better executive incentives and attractions, and their greater participation in dealing with social perils in the postindustrial society will woo into industry some of the best civil servants. The better grade of government people, some previously alienated from business, might see new bases from which they could work for the public good, actually accomplish something, and make a lot of money doing it. This effect isn't certain, but it is a possibility worth watching for.

It is tempting to walk you through the many other functions and concepts on which our business world runs and relate them all to the supercorporation. But it must be clear that supers will strike and change nearly every part of corporate life, as well as the personal lives of the tens of millions of people who will be working in the world of the postindustrial corporations. The next chapter deals with one of the more exciting changes in the business environment that supers are likely to bring about: the use of venture management.

8

VENTURE MANAGEMENT, A NEW/OLD ACTIVITY

TODAY, AND EVEN MORE IN THE FUTURE, we have something quite special in venture management. In its new, formal version, venture management is nothing less than a successful corporate means of installing entrepreneurial talent and creativity where corporate bureaucracy had plodded before.

The early applications of venture management are already working well, producing new businesses on a fairly dependable schedule for some 25 to 35 large U.S. corporations, and for some corporations in other countries. To emphasize, over 50 U.S. corporations already have started formal entrepreneurial departments. Each is set up and intensely motivated to identify new profit opportunities, evaluate them, develop the best ones, and build them into viable new businesses. We have three to six years' experience to date for a number of users. If the new, organized venture management departments can continue to produce new businesses and profit centers over longer periods of time, as I predict, then venture management will be one of the great and governing assets of the large corporation, at least until 1990.

Before I relate the venture management activity to the particular needs of supercorporations, more perspective will be helpful. First, a definition: Venture management is the formal organization and operation of a new business development enterprise within the structure of the large corporation.

The title of this chapter calls venture management a new/old activity. Stockholders may assume that a lot of corporate effort normally goes into the development of new businesses, products, and services. In many companies this assumption is fulfilled—up to a point, but that point is a limited one.

It has previously been noted (in Part One) that as it now stands, the record of new product and new service development by conventional corporations and the swinging conglomerates is generally abysmal. Procter & Gamble, General Foods, Sears, Roebuck, a few large banks, and a scattering of others are brilliant exceptions. By and large, we know that the infant mortality of new products and new services for conventional corporations is something like 80 percent. No one has figured out the total costs of such a performance for the economy as a whole, but they must be astronomical.

Back to the stockholders, who naturally assume that their corporations are constantly working on new growth opportunities. They are, but we see that managements usually need more capability than has been applied. At this juncture, the new/old activity of venture management is increasingly entering the corporate structure and process.

Given this need for a booster shot for new growth activities, a further description of venture management is needed to show the connection between venture management and the new supercorporations.

Venture Management Today

As practiced by an increasing number of our largest conventional corporations, the venture management activity is organized and operated as a separate unit of the corporation. The venture management unit is usually located in corporate headquarters and reports to a senior executive. Thus, this separate venture management department is at least on a plane organizationally with marketing, finance, and other similar departments or activities.

The boundary between venture management and more familiar corporate departments requires some drawing. Venture management is principally the entrepreneurial function in the corporation. As such, it helps set the growth goals, makes the new-business studies, picks the best new profit possibilities, screens them, chooses a few, and spearheads their development into significant profit centers. Centering on entrepreneurial activities, the venture management function in most conventional corporations is not the same as the R&D function; rather, venture management taps traditional R&D departments to find new venture ideas and to get help in evaluating and developing new venture opportunities. A similar relationship usually exists between venture management and the new-product department.

The venture management department also works in tandem with the acquisition, or corporate development, activity. Venture managers can not only glean new venture ideas from acquisition experts, they can also determine with these experts whether the various parts of a new venture can better be acquired or internally developed.

A few more relationships will box the compass of venture management as it is most capably pursued today. Venture management has both inputs to and outputs from the corporate or long-range planning section of the corporation. It presents to corporate planning its expectations on the nature, size, timing, and other requirements of its actual and projected ventures. In turn, venture management receives outlines of other corporate and divisional activities that could help or harm the venture management work, as well as confirmation of venture management's requested charter, guidelines, and resources.

Finally, venture management is not a substitute for the financial group of the corporation, but interfaces with it. In addition to specific budgetary and cash matters, venture management receives from the financial area (or from corporate planning) the financial parameters and standards that are to govern all ventures. The potential and actual results of new ventures, in turn, can affect considerably the financial standards and results of the corporation as a whole.

From these and other intracorporate relationships, it is clear that the venture management activity is formal and thoroughly organized. Without venture management, the entrepreneurial function per se almost never turns up on organization charts, and is therefore often fragmented or even entirely absent from new product and other growth efforts.

A study I directed in 1970 of the 100 largest U.S. industrial corporations found that over 40 of them are already practicing venture management in some form. In one way or another their venture management is a distinct part of the business enterprise—not just regular R&D, not the normal new product development, not just the familiar acquisitions team. Rather, their venture management departments are separate, organized groups that exist to find new—and often unrelated—businesses, and to put their corporations profitably into some of those businesses.

A handful of companies (3M, for example) are already recognized for their flair and adroitness in this, one of the most difficult of all corporate activities. Others—Monsanto, Owens-Illinois, General Mills, and Du Pont—are also realizing good returns on their investments in venture management.

Venture Management in Supercorporations

In supercorporations, there will be two differences in venture management. First, it will usually be central to the entire corporation, whereas venture management in a number of conventional corporations is still experimental and often viewed suspiciously by traditional managers and departments. Second, venture management will be nearly universally adopted by the supercorporations.

What supports these predicted differences? The ways venture management works are custom-made for the super-growth needs of the new giants. These ways include better means of providing the supers with the rare people who have entrepreneurial talents and better means of helping these people to be productive.

While almost every executive tells you that all his problems are people problems, the people problems of entrepreneurialism and of the venture management function are more difficult than some others. Consider the familiar tendency of people in large conventional corporations to bog down in bureaucracy and caution, to try to keep their noses clean, and to avoid rocking the boat. Executives who emphasize such a safe and orderly progression up the seniority ladder show nothing of the entrepreneur. In fact, most large corporations attract few entrepreneurs in the first place, and keep even fewer of them. People who want to start their own businesses usually manage to do so, but not within the large conventional corporation. One of the principal undocumented reasons for the slow growth—or slow decline—of so many large conventional corporations is a scarcity of real live business builders—entrepreneurs.

For large conventional corporations that both need business builders and also repel them, the venture management function is one of the few workable solutions. Venture management provides the adventure that the entrepreneur requires. In addition, some venture management setups already are offering venture managers large amounts of extra or contingent compensation. This uncharacteristically bold compensation gives the entrepreneur who successfully starts a new profit center the "piece of the action" that he demands.

One of the reasons why venture management will see its greatest flowering in supercorporations is that the super will be far better equipped as a home for entrepreneurs than are most conventional corporations. In terms of business-building opportunities and substantial special compensation, the super can shine. It will have a far more intense imperative to grow, and it will have notably more flexibility for bestowing upon the extraordinary producer his extraordinary rewards.

Thus, highly motivated people will make the order-of-magnitude difference in effectiveness between venture management and the typical bureaucratic new product and new service function.

An example of venture management today should provide a peek at what the supercorporations will be doing with this growth function. I refer to that fast-growing European commercial banker, Dow Chemical. Who? It has somehow escaped the notice of many businessmen that Dow Chemical owns and runs a multinational commercial bank in Europe, with total assets exceeding $300 million. Dow has reported that this commercial banking business helped underwrite 36 corporate and 18 government financings in one 18-month period, and that it is building toward the 14 percent return on investment that is the Dow criterion for all its profit centers.

It is not such a long and unpredictable way from Dow's Midland, Michigan, world headquarters to its Zurich bank's headquarters, if we realize that Dow espouses venture management. This Dow venture touches the essence of new ventures for large companies: putting massive resources together with a growth-motivated team of corporate entrepreneurs, and having the courage to go where the ventures lead.

In this case Dow started in 1965 with excess cash of $23 million to invest in Europe for a period of about five years. At that time no bank would consider such an investment service. Upon further analysis, Dow spotted a venture opportunity. Since 1965 Dow Banking of Zurich has earned millions each year in profits. In 1972 Dow Chemical sold 25 percent of its bank to Japan's Fuji Bank for some $14 million. This suggests that Dow Chemical's original investment in its European banking venture more than doubled in value in seven years. Because venture management is supposed to produce profitable new growth enterprises by plan—not by luck—it is instructive to see that Dow Chemical has successfully gone into additional banking ventures overseas which include buying 45 percent of Banco Cidade de São Paulo, Brazil and participating in this bank's opening of banks in Grand Cayman and Zurich.

Implications for the Business Community

The superb use of venture management by supercorporations will have many significant effects on business in the United States. First, there will be hundreds, if not thousands, of new and upgraded venture management positions near the tops of the supers, semisupers, and their emulators. In fact, the future top managements of large corporations, conventional and super, are likely to be enriched by graduates of the venture management teams being moved into the highest levels of management.

Personal and corporate stakes will become much greater. There will be more and bigger personal successes through the expansion of venture management, just as there will be more and bigger failures. Concurrently, the often monolithic compensation and benefit programs of large corporations will be shattered by the painful and complicated adoption of entrepreneurial rewards for entrepreneurial results.

As for the mass of other corporate employees, they will be faced with demands for more creative, less bureaucratic responses to the venture management function. Boredom should be a little less common for the nonventure groups.

In addition to other changes in competition because of the supers, their embrace of venture management is likely to reduce markedly the "me-too" kind of competition that is all too characteristic of so-called growth efforts. On the other hand, governments should expect more competition to be created by supers and other large corporations as venture management spreads. The multiple and successful competitive attacks on the parcel post and other services of the U.S. Postal Service are a plain sign of what is coming: a reversal of government in business, with business taking lucrative bites out of services formerly provided only by the government. One portion of this expected competition is explored in Part Three, Chapter 14.

Finally, there should be valid, though not traceable, increments in corporate efficiency through the decline of the conventionally inefficient new product development efforts and the rise of progressively more astute venture management.

The first two major changes in business due to supercorporations— new organizational structures and greater use of venture management—are alone enough to change the corporate landscape. Three more such changes remain to be explored, the next being the supercorporation attempt at managing people.

9

A SUPERCORPORATION ATTEMPT at MANAGING PEOPLE

PRODUCTIVITY IS A SUBJECT of abiding interest. It underlies our ability, or inability, to fund the staggering costs of ever more elaborate attempts to solve our social problems. At the same time, the productivity of people has become more important and difficult to improve, as every new model of "automated" wonder machine and system is found to be people dependent. Contrary to some futurists, I believe that this persistent people-centered technology should be with us to and after 1990. Its productivity is as vital in the executive suites, which use or misuse the cleverest computer systems, as it is in entry-level laboring jobs.

The management of people and their productivity at all levels will be one of the toughest problems of supercorporations, in common with all other kinds of groups of people who are supposed to work together. I am not certain that supers will do this thankless task better than other companies, but there is a possibility that they will. If so, their solutions will not come from the factory floor, nor from foundations and labor organizations, nor from government. Rather, we can expect the attempts and successes of supercorporations to flow outward from their managements. One of my least supported conjectures, but an important one, is that most gains in people productivity will have to start with obviously better productivity and attitudes within management ranks, and later spread to lower level workers in the office, factory, mine, oilfield, farm, transportation, and other services.

In any outward-spreading waves of improving people productivity, supers and others will have to be doing much more to rework horrifying attitudes than to upgrade operating methods and techniques. If this management-outward approach should work, it would be one of the few approaches capable of beginning to redeem the extreme anti-productivity attitudes of so much of our workforce—as wonderfully recorded in Studs Terkel's *Working*.[1]

To address the convoluted problems of people management, attitudes, and productivity, we start with the collections of theories and the flood of words that attempt to deal with one of man's oldest problems: how to organize, motivate, lead, direct, and control people in groups. Excepting the precious few men and women who manage corporate people surpassingly well, the generality of managers need help, and this is only occasionally forthcoming.

This chapter has three clear messages. First, there is no general theory and no general practice of dependably effective people management in large corporations. Second, the cornucopia of newer theories and concepts, often preached with old-time fervor, either are not the answer or have not yet been received by line managers as the answer. Third, supercorporations will inherently be equipped to discover better answers, test them, and use them more productively than conventional corporations.

There is a place for faith in all this—the faith that a new kind of corporation will by 1990 make a difference in this awesomely difficult area. The basis for this faith is, naturally, the essence of the supercorporation itself. The least tangible aspect of the supers will be the aura and atmosphere of growing through meeting extreme challenges. This super ambience may trigger a chain of reactions strong enough to move executives and employees—as a group—to breakthroughs in people management.

Those who have not been managers may not grasp the extreme malaise and the intense apathy of today's employees. Their problems seem to have been outshouted by the spectacular actions of racial minorities and others. However, employee problems are widespread.

[1] New York: Pantheon, 1974.

They are one of the most civil forms of the general social disaffection.

What might supercorporations and those who follow them do about this condition as it comes to work every morning? Corporate managers have already tried many methods, especially with executives and non-union employees. Four that have been quite extensively applied are compensation investment, including incentives such as stock options; participative management, including management by objectives; sensitivity training; and organization development.

These and other methods have not been sufficient. But even more alarming is the possibility that not enough young people will be interested in becoming corporate managers. We will note this problem and its relation to supercorporations and then cover two other points: a small but promising solution to some aspects of people problems and the potential nature of supercorporations' efforts in people management.

A Shortage of Managers

Although it seems incredible, the possibility exists that literally there may not be enough managers to man our corporate executive positions, starting in the late 1970s. If the problem is allowed to develop completely, two of its multiple results would strike supercorporations just as they are coming into their own: first, an absolute shortage of managers, leading to the inevitable curbing of otherwise attainable growth; and second, a slashing of the effectiveness of any otherwise workable programs devised by supercorporations for enhancing their people management.

Dr. John B. Miner, research professor of management at Georgia State University, first called my attention to the problem, and he has since published a book on it, *The Human Constraint*.[2] He says that as long ago as the mid-1960s, the motivation and attitudes of business students began signaling a deep-seated shift away from those usually needed to be a corporate manager. To consider this matter, you need to accept the validity of psychological testing methods for identifying motivations and for relating an individual's motivations to those gener-

[2] Washington, D.C.: Bureau of National Affairs, 1974.

ally required for success in corporate management. Certainly there are many executives who do not accept the reliability of any form of psychological testing for business purposes. This is a moment, however, for skeptics to join believers in order to assess this potential management shortage.

In addition to Dr. Miner, other researchers have come up with similar findings, independently derived. At the Harvard Business School, Lewis Ward and Anthony Athos have been studying the attitudes of students since 1962. At Harvard, of all places, they find declining interest in large corporations and lessened motivation for managerial positions in them. These observers, too, are raising the specter of ". . . the slow starvation of large corporations for lack of future managerial talent." [3]

Dr. Miner also has proposed two possible means of preventing this problem from becoming epidemic. (The problem, and any solutions, are deeply involved in the subjects of manpower planning and programming in Chapter 10.) He suggests that the large corporation can employ both "input" and "input improving" strategies. Input strategies would call for more intensive recruiting of the potentially shrinking number of managerially motivated candidates. This recruiting would include the traditional sources and candidates, plus the needed types of women and noncollege candidates. Input improving strategies rest on as yet early and experimental evidence that managerial motivation can in fact be taught in certain kinds of lecture and discussion programs.

Even the possibility of a shortage of capable women and men who are motivationally willing and able to manage is tremendously alarming to those who do manage people. To the extent that this problem is not averted, the presence of supercorporations, as people-rich companies, will make the people-poor ones still poorer. For whoever wants to manage, the supercorporation should provide the most attractive framework of company growth potential, rapid personal advancement, unusual management development programs, and the like. The extra attractiveness of the new supers and their emulators, coupled with a tight supply of managers, could add to the squeeze on postindustrial conventional corporations.

---

[3] *Student Expectations of Corporate Life: Implications for Management Recruiting* (Boston: Division of Research, Harvard Business School, 1972), p. 81.

A Possible Solution to Some People Problems

Corporations have, as a group, tried everything from peremptory dismissals to sincere attempts at personal counseling and aid to handle their people problems. Few, if any, executives have been satisfied with their company's results, or even satisfied that the right methods have been found.

One exception is the Utah Copper Division of Kennecott Copper. For over four years, the division has made its "Insight" service available to its 8,000 employees. The service was originally built around one psychiatric worker, his secretary, and two part-time assistants, and had a total annual budget of about $30,000. Insight provides a highly personalized, confidential counseling and referral service for employees and dependents. The service is available seven days a week, 24 hours a day. It seems to have been unique, especially in precluding any stigma from attaching to the users or to the program itself.

In the first 20 months, 1,053 Utah Copper employees and 1,180 dependents voluntarily solicited help. Results have been better than in most other corporate programs. In an alcoholism group of 37, 12 enrolled in a treatment program for an average of 12.5 months. Absences decreased 50 percent, and measurable benefits costs dropped from $180 to $85 per month. In a second group, this one of 87 chronic absentees, 67 improved their attendance, with an overall improvement of 44 percent. In addition to reducing alcoholism and absenteeism, Insight has intervened in 15 suicide attempts, dealt with racial discrimination, helped obtain pregnancy tests, and so on.

Equally important are the people's reactions. A representative of the union local in Salt Lake City says that some union members needing help will go to Insight rather than to their own stewards, who are encouraged by the unions to help members with personal problems. It has been reported that the 19 unions in the Utah Copper Division are boosters of Insight.

At least three things can definitely be said about Insight in its early life: It worked, in terms of the volume of response; one of every eight employees, plus another 1,200 dependents, sought help in the first 20 months. It thus gives evidence of helping to solve numbers of personal problems. And it has gained and held the confidence of five often-opposed groups: top management, labor organizations, individual employees and dependents, staff specialists, and line management.

It would be ironic if the heartless, dehumanizing, excessively materialistic giant corporation were to become a high-volume, high-quality, highly personal avenue of confidential help and counsel. But it just could be so. We may know in about five years.

This kind of service faces many hazards. But its early performance has been promising, and other corporations have already begun to emulate this first experiment. If, against odds, Insight and similar services can become widespread, we would then have one of the few workable keys to unlocking the dilemmas of people management in large corporations.

Supercorporations and People Management

Having observed the chilling possibility of a dearth of managers and the heartening possibility of corporate counsel and aid in personal problems, we must now consider how supercorporations, at their projected best, will deal with the whole range of people problems. Will supers be thwarted by an inability to solve the problems we have collected under the heading of "people management"? Will they work around such basic problems by better adaptations of today's conventional means? Or will they somehow achieve the highly unlikely goal of creating real breakthroughs in managing people in large groups?

My conclusion, in a field where most conclusions have been wrong, is that supercorporations will almost certainly handle people management well enough to permit their required growth, and they may also find and prove a few new answers of value to themselves and others.

For the safest of our projections on supercorporations in people management, we go back to some of the oldest concepts and methods, which will almost certainly be used by this new kind of corporate being. One of the old concepts is leadership—rare these days, but still workable, when most of the newer, fancier programs are unreliable. The second of the old concepts is getting and keeping quality people, not in every position, but more than one's accidental share. The third is strong incentive and other compensation.

It seems childishly simple to talk of putting these three concepts together to build something special. Any freshman could think of it.

But the IBMs and Xeroxes are so embarrassingly few that more than a freshman must be needed to put them all together. Take the case of IBM. Many computer technicians have been saying for years that IBM has not always had the most cost effective computers—nor the most key patents, nor the lowest prices, and so on. But IBM has had the best in management and marketing. And it has been one of the biggest winners in the history of our industrial society, with more than 60 percent of its market and with superb growth.

With so much sophistication around us, it is easy to overlook the elemental fact that IBM and other growth leaders have played a great game of fundamental management in the specified areas of leadership, better people, and strong compensation. Delta Air Lines and Gould, Inc. are two other outstanding companies whose people-management approaches are too infrequently emulated.

The supercorporations will do no less, the opinion of Frederick Herzberg notwithstanding. (He believes that money does not motivate.) Look at it this way. If companies like International Utilities or ITT, which are already achieving above-average growth, take on the further characteristics of supercorporations, they are going to end up employing marvelously well the old fundamentals of people management. For it was these fundamentals that helped them succeed in the first place.

This is pretty trite stuff. No buzz words, no advanced management fabrications, no discoveries in the behavioral sciences. No, we are basing our first categorical prediction of supercorporations' success in people management on calculably better performance of the tried and true fundamentals.

Of course, supercorporations will also provide new arenas for experimentation and development of new methods for people management. A large company that has three to six top executives in the office of the chairman and is very hungry for ways to perpetuate its compounded growth rate of 10 percent can find some units in which to make controlled experiments over an extended period.

Accordingly, the second projection about supercorporations in people management is that they will have greater freedom to try the far-out, the new, the chancy. Lesser companies, scrimping along on narrow margins and declining earnings per share, might botch it if they tried, say, organization development. The further point is that few of the lesser companies would dare to experiment, whereas supers and some semisupers will have developed a climate that allows them to dare a lot.

Beginning with the fact that there are few hard answers to people problems and incessant claims to have found them, we can project the nature of supercorporation experimentation. Every line manager, and every financial executive, has been bombarded with extravagant claims of the return on investment to be had from this or that answer to problems of people management. Line and finance people cannot know from their own experience which of the claims can be accepted as true. Take organization development (OD) again as an example.

Some of the keenest specialists are on the pro side. On the con side are the naturally skeptical businessmen—most of us—as well as some unconvinced specialists. One experienced observer has gone so far as to say that a widespread use of OD-like participative management would put U.S. industry at a competitive disadvantage in world markets. Another, Dr. Abraham Zaleznik, has scathingly characterized some forms of group development as "a search for love through membership," and as an essentially unsound view of human relationships in business.[4]

Now, enter a few supercorporations, with their driving need to find better means for improving people's performance; their secure status, from which they can dare new things; and the ambitions of their venture management departments to package their in-house experience and market it profitably. These supercorporations, having also the wealth to fund the needed work, are going to give OD and many other people-management hypotheses the workout of their lives.

If and when several supercorporations undertake massive experiments or development efforts over periods of years, the results will carry weight with many line managers throughout the postindustrial business world. If the supers can sharpen motivation, stoke up participation, enliven communication, and so on, then many will follow— just as they will abandon the supers' methods if they prove unsuccessful. So the supers will likely become the biggest and most remarked people-management laboratories ever. Behavioral scientists, social psychologists, personnel researchers and specialists, and all the other specialists will find the supers holding their feet to the fire of substan-

4 *Business Week* (March 10, 1973), pp. 18, 20.

tial investigation. We might even have more data and less discussion, which by itself would be a kind of millennium.

Finally, a speculation on top of a speculation. Whatever the values of today's old and new concepts of people management, these concepts are unlikely to be more than partial solutions, at best. Our double speculation is that supercorporations, or at least some of them, will be the source of some state-of-the-art breakthroughs in people management. Just as Kennecott, not a super, created its unique Insight program for its employees and dependents, so also, we are guessing, some supercorporations will invent some other excellent solutions. There is no direct proof, but this speculation is easily one of the most provocative of all those we have made regarding supers and people management.

Thus, one of the means by which supercorporations can reach their high growth—provided that no overwhelming shortage of managers develops—is by managing people better. At minimum, they will provide superior leadership, hire proportionally much more capable employees, and use far stronger compensation programs, including very high incentives.

Further, the supers can make additional solutions for themselves and others for reasons inherent in their nature, such as their extreme need for better performance, their practical and psychological climate that allows—or sparks—the daring use of new and initially strange theories and methods, and their continuing interest in packaging their internal systems and programs as new ventures and additional profit centers. Moreover, the likelihood exists that some supers will act as oversized laboratories, testing various methods of people management, and will provide valuable conclusions from such otherwise rare experiments. More speculatively, they may even create solutions not yet conceived today. In all, supercorporations will have a profound effect on people-management problems and solutions, and in some cases may be the bête noire of some widely espoused concepts of the 1960s and early 1970s.

10

MANPOWER PLANNING, A TOOL for SUPERCORPORATIONS

SINCE MANPOWER PLANNING is less than a leading subject, why dwell on it here? Simply because we are concerned especially with the impact of supercorporations on people in business, and manpower planning is one of the most relevant functions. Also, if my forecasts are correct, manpower planning will have a lot to do with the development of supers, and vice versa. First a note on what manpower planning involves.

Like the long-standing informal and ineffectual venture management situations, traditional efforts in manpower planning have proved less and less sufficient for businesses that are growing and changing. It was classic in the last century for the office boy to become president. When, however, International Utilities, a prospective supercorporation, adds $313 million in sales in just one year (1972–1973) and $13.2 million in profits in the same year, then it cannot wait for the office boy to become president or even to become a senior systems analyst. Rather, the immediate task of manpower planning is to provide means for filling the currently needed positions. At the same time, its longer term task is to ensure that the company will have the senior systems analysts it will need—possibly by including a career path for the office boy.

The newness of the new version of manpower planning is surprising. A study I directed in 1971 of over 200 large companies found that two-thirds had had a formal, organized manpower-planning function for fewer than five years. One in five companies studied had been at it for less than one year. Evidently, most of the manpower planning that will be done in large corporations has not even been started yet. Conversations with managers in charge of manpower planning in a basic metal company and in a pharmaceuticals company, for instance, disclosed that the assignment of their positions and titles was as far as the manpower-planning process had then progressed. The "manpower planning managers" had, for a time, been shifted to other duties, while keeping intact their forward-looking titles.

Nevertheless, three essentials of manpower planning are especially relevant to supercorporations and their effects on business people: the special usefulness of computers, manpower forecasting, and the hopeful world of manpower programming.

Computers and Confidential Personnel Data

The idea that computers will be especially useful in manpower planning should provoke at least a mild storm. The dehumanizing of our society already includes putting people onto computer punch cards and tapes. Must we suffer still more of this in postindustrial society because of supercorporations?

Paradoxically, the computer is more likely to be a liberating force than an imprisoning one. Properly approached, the computerizing of business personnel data makes possible (1) an extension of the range and variety of data that can be kept; (2) a degree of analysis and cross-checking of personnel data that was never seriously attempted in the era of file cabinets and green eyeshades; (3) and an ease and timeliness in the availability of data and analyses that have also been unattainable, regardless of cost.

With these three advances some practical and humane things are beginning to happen. First, more people are being considered for more opportunities because the corporation no longer relies on the imperfect recollections of a few busy men. Second, manpower data are more fully used in all kinds of management decisions because they have been collected into one place for the first time. Third, the enormous costs of compensation and benefits plans are being managed more efficiently through extensive analyses not previously attempted.

I think that supercorporations will be the biggest and most adroit users of computers. They should lead in applying them to personnel data, hopefully without more dehumanizing effects.

Manpower Forecasting

A second aspect of manpower planning that intersects the coming of the supercorporation is the increasing availability of usable manpower forecasts. Large conventional corporations have regularly used economic forecasts, but have usually had to step back to thinly supported guesses regarding their future manpower situations. This has been costly, in that employee compensation of all types is one of the largest costs in all companies. However, now that the basic data have been computerized, a few corporations with a serious interest in forecasting are beginning to plan for facilities, set levels of subcontracting requirements, control uses of overtime, plan layoffs, monitor manpower costs, and project replacements for managers.

The supercorporation can be expected to use more than its share of such forecasts. One of the characteristics necessary for a conventional corporation to become a super is a greater flexibility in moving into and out of products, services, and other ventures. These decisions are ultimately judgmental. Since forecasts can reduce dependence on guesswork, they will be called for with increasing frequency.

Consider the unsuccessful attempt by Gulf + Western to take control of A&P, the large supermarket chain. If either G + W or A&P could have forecast manpower situations, their attacking and defending strategies could have been stronger and would probably have been quite different. For example, either side could have benefited from knowing the specific effects on manpower costs of increasing, or decreasing, the number of A&P stores by, say, 20 percent; or the cost effects of using more, or less, part-time help; or the influence on profits of upgrading, or downgrading, the quality of employees in a dozen common positions that employ some 10,000 people in A&P; or the possible results of a major change in incentive compensation for store managers and division managers. Although this example is hypothetical, it illustrates the hard-nosed decisions that can be made, with better batting averages, by the faster moving and more demanding supercorporations through use of manpower forecasting.

Manpower Programming

Manpower programming, called above a hopeful world, is the part of manpower planning that devises the means (that is, the programs) for accomplishing specified changes in a company's manpower situation. It provides programs for a gamut of activities—supplying the needed numbers and types of employees, developing them, promoting them, and so forth.

Four recognized, although not yet widely used applications of manpower programming are career pathing, career guidance, fast-track programs, and executive-replacement planning.

CAREER PATHING

Career pathing is the plotting of alternative routes by which individuals progress through a series of positions to an attainable intermediate or final position. An oversimplified career path for a marketing executive in a division of a diversified textile company might start with the position of sales trainee and move, if the individual succeeds along the way, through salesman, regional sales manager, product manager, assistant national sales manager, national sales manager, and so on. Career pathing has not been widely used, for it strikes many line executives as either documenting the obvious or thrashing around among a number of unplannable alternative paths. There is not yet a large body of successful experience in career pathing, as there is in, say, the training of salesmen in product knowledge.

Supercorporations would be especially aware that career pathing is not an end in itself. For them, career pathing is one of the possible ingredients in trying to attract certain types of high-performance individuals into a company and trying to keep them there as well-motivated and rising employees. It is also a way of working out the best trade-offs between an individual's business and personal interests and the immediate and expected personnel needs of the company.

In the experience of one "Big Eight" public accounting firm, 25 percent or more of its "professional" employees are business consultants of some kind, not CPAs. Because the route to the top in a public accounting firm is through the audit and tax paths, a sticky career-pathing problem arises. Some of the business consultants may become CPAs and get back into the mainstream. A few others may rise high enough within the business consulting division to have an acceptable path. But what of the others? Probably the majority of those in the business consulting arms are not entirely clear or satisfied as to whether they have a long-term future in a public accounting firm. The plotting of career paths does not invent opportunities that do not exist. But it may be one productive means of identifying more or better career opportunities in what could otherwise be considered a dead-end affiliation.

Whatever the value and future of career pathing in conventional corporations, conglomerates, and growth companies, this process will become a different ball game as supercorporations come into being. On the one hand, the supers may find that career pathing is simply not a useful enough process to be justified. If this should be the conclusion, career pathing would be met with further negative reactions in other types of corporations partly because of the fad syndrome.

On the other hand, the chance is about equal that career pathing will be adopted by supercorporations with suitable modifications. One of the characteristics of supers is that they will move into and out of profit centers, geographic areas, job assignments, functional activities, investments, and so on with greater aplomb than most other corporations. It is clear that the normal, longer term career path is more likely to be interrupted and radically changed in the supers. Individuals may judge such interruptions and radical changes to be either favorable or unfavorable to them. But even those who accept the sudden shifts will want some personal and financial cushioning of the jolts, plus some tangible, believable assurance that the next unsought bounce will not necessarily be their last in the company.

For this latter need, a super adaptation of career pathing would supply a partial help to employer and employee. Instead of relying on an arm around the shoulder or an extra-long luncheon, both parties could consult the preexisting career paths that lie near the employee's current crossroads. The very fact of the preexisting career paths, if previously followed at all, would have a quieting effect on the individual's apprehensions, while supplying some concrete ideas to a harassed boss who has more problems than he can juggle. The scenario for career pathing in supercorporations brings this modification into play.

In contrast with the obvious and direct paths more common to the conventional corporation, the career paths of the super would have more varied branchings. For example, the assistant division manager in the leasing division does not want to go with that division when it is sold off to a financial services corporation; or else the selling corporation is loath to lose a real comer. A preexisting set of career paths showing achievable but imaginative career steps for middle-level financial executives would make a useful difference. Whereas the conventional corporation in this scene might portray most progressions in controllership and treasury posts, the super might have been forced to add some career paths into division general management, overseas positions, venture management, special corporate staff assignments, and positions in its other financially related service businesses, such as the captive consumer finance company, the partially owned merchant bank in Europe, or the mortgage banking affiliate that supports its condominium development business.

This wider career-pathing scope implies some other things, too—especially that a new breed of aggressive and flexible executive will be in great demand by the aggressive and flexible new supercorporations. At this moment, let us limit ourselves to the immediate matter of career pathing. It may be concluded that if supercorporations do not kill career pathing because of inappropriateness for their special needs, they may find this part of the manpower-programming process useful and may bend its normal applications to their different needs.

CAREER GUIDANCE

Plainly related to any career pathing that may exist is career guidance, the service of assisting an employee to make career decisions that fit, as well as possible, the needs of both himself and his company. This service, as is the case with certain other corporate activities, may be suspect as an establishment plot, and a conflict of interest, to boot. Many employees, including top executives, feel that they have the scars to prove that the corporation is unable or unwilling to look at the individual's side of the situation. This is all too easy to accept as the whole of the matter.

In a fast-paced corporation of 10,000 or 60,000 employees, the individual can probably benefit from some corporate inputs before he makes his career plans and decisions. Information that is tilted toward the corporation's advantage, especially when so recognized, is better than no information at all. The idea that one must accept a move or be forever downgraded in management's eyes, a frequent complaint of employees, may not always be the trap it is perceived to be. With an organized and thought-through process of career guidance, this move-or-lose shibboleth could at least be explored. If this widely rumored policy should not actually be governing, the individual could learn, through the career-guidance process, that he need not feel trapped, because he can choose other alternatives that still fit with the company's interests in him.

The reader inexperienced in handling people may assume that all these things are usually taken care of anyway, and that a career-guidance function is boondoggling and redundant. We do not have a full answer, so a partial answer must suffice. The mails and files of over 300 executive recruiting firms, containing hundreds of thousands of furtively sent résumés, are a clear hint that all is not well in employee relations generally and in career guidance specifically. Career guidance is not worse off than other people-oriented functions. Rather it is one of those that the distant viewer assumes has been decently handled for years. Actually, the experience of employees ranges from magnificent concern and follow-through by their boss to impersonal indifference to their career problems. George Bernard Shaw said in his play *The Devil's Disciple,* "The worst sin towards our fellow creatures is not to hate them, but to be indifferent to them." This applies also to the contemporary corporate handling of some employees, and brings us right to the supercorporations.

The supercorporations will realize that the above-average management cadre they require will not be attracted, motivated, and held automatically or solely by the force of their leaders' personalities. After initial disappointments with the limitations of toothsome compensation packages, there will be an organized search for something else or something more. One of the answers will probably be found in manpower planning and in its component function, manpower programming. Within manpower programming, career guidance is likely to be useful.

Here, again, the super can be expected to make some local variations on the scattered existing patterns in conventional and other corporations. A reasonable possibility is that, way back in the super's recruiting process, there will have been enticing words said about "human resource management" and "manpower programming." Then, if there is any actual backup for these brave words, the super-corporation will have given its personnel people a few years to work out some programs that lead toward tangible results. At this point, the predicted changes, rapid and abrupt, will be hitting a lot of those carefully recruited overachievers.

With no one process or tool being adequate in itself, the supers may well turn to a form of career guidance uniquely their own. They could, for example, produce an amalgam of in-house guidance by per-sonnel staffers, add line-manager participation when it can be gotten, and beef up the mix by using an outside service group for the top 100 or 2,000 most valuable employees. In this instance an outside group of unusually high quality might be retained over a period of several years. It would either audit the career-guidance process and report on results or perform assigned aspects of the career-guidance process, particularly filling gaps left by the company's own service groups and line managers.

Here, as elsewhere, the outlines of the future are indistinct. Some of the newest and brightest ideas either will not be anticipated at all or will be seen later by other observers. The inside/outside setup, just hypothesized, will have to stand as a tangible example of the possible use of career guidance by supercorporations, and of the greater use and special twists they are likely to provide.

Fast-Track Programs

The third manpower programming function, fast-track programs, is such a natural one for supercorporations that caution is indicated. Fast-track programs identify those women and men within the company who have unusually high potential and provide them with accelerated development programs and job opportunities. Such programs are not widely used, even in large corporations that consider themselves ad-vanced in enlightened management of their people.

The hazards of fast-track programs are obvious. One may pick wrongly his young tigers. Or he may do a poorer job of develop-ment—an imperfect art—than if the career were not all so planned and fixed. The other valuable employees may be more alienated by a fast-track program than by age-old informal means of moving some employees along faster than others. In an age of aggressive recruiting—some would say pirating—of highly valuable people from one company to another, it might even simplify the recruiter's job if he were able to identify someone else's stable of fast-track men and women and court them intensively.

There is, to date, no permanent resolution of the debate on whether or not to have a formal, organized fast-track program, or whether to play it by ear. There may never be a consensus. The question turns partly on individual styles of management, and management style is never going to be stereotyped in a supercorporation. For some managers, at least, the fast-track program is likely to seem a smart way to attract and hold young superstars, without too many offsetting disadvantages. For these managers, the fast-track program will become a part of manpower programming, within the manpower-planning function.

Will the supercorporation make any difference in fast-track programming? Perhaps so. Whatever their individual natures, supers will tend, primarily because of their greater diversity, to have more profit centers and other defined responsibility centers than conventional corporations of comparable size. The previously predicted coming of age of make-versus-buy decisions in supercorporations will turn the once-typical morass of corporate, divisional, and subsidiary staff services into a tighter matrix of planned performance units. With more positions that are genuinely measurable, and actively measured, there will be plenty of changes in management and managers.

One relevant change is that more fast-track women and men will have more opportunities, sooner, to show their stuff—in their actual, measurable performance, not just in their genial personality or clever political footwork. One contribution of those supercorporations that actually try the fast-track idea will be an increase in the quantity and the measurability of fast-track programs, and thus in their knowledge of who their best people really are.

EXECUTIVE-REPLACEMENT PLANNING

The fourth of the manpower-programming functions to be considered in terms of the supercorporations' effects is executive-replacement planning. As with other subjects, I must leave out most of the juice, including only enough to indicate the interrelationships between supers and the subject at hand. Thus, for brevity, this discussion of executive-replacement planning leaves out far more than it tells.

Does the coming of the supercorporation look as though it would change the current executive-replacement process very much? Perhaps not. One can assume that nearly all the supers will employ the function formally and will work hard on it during most regimes.

But there is another possibility. The likely use by a number of supercorporations of the office of the chairman as their top management organizational structure will increase their needs for top executives. The addition of one to five top people to the top management level of a corporation may seem numerically picayune. But anyone who has unsuccessfully or successfully recruited even one chief executive knows of the extreme difficulty of picking the right person out of a number of wonderfully presentable candidates. The office of the chairman is a potential source of more than proportional needs for executive replacements, and therefore another extra burden on the executive-replacement process for supercorporations.

These further characteristics of supercorporations also suggest that they will be more pressed than other types of corporations to find replacements for their executives: the establishment of joint ventures and multiple captives; the acquisition of more companies than do most other large corporations; and the participation in miscellaneous partial ownerships of still other entities. Add to this the possible acceleration of executive musical chairs through well-timed fast-track programs, and we have a new order of need for effective executive replacement.

What will supercorporations do? Two guesses may be ventured. Supers will probably hit executive-replacement planning by the well-worn device of elevating it—along with other people-management functions—a few organizational levels above its usual lodging. The squeaking wheel gets the grease and the elevation usually works. Some supers can be expected to move executive replacement right into the office of the chairman.

When this happens we can expect that one of the members of that office will be given major responsibility for this and other people-management functions. This could be a double bonus, in that this executive can be expected to have had heavy line experience in getting tough jobs done. (It is no criticism of many personnel executives to observe that they have not had such high-level line experience.)

To summarize, it is fair to predict that supercorporations will stamp both quantitative and qualitative changes on today's theoretical and practical versions of people management generally and manpower programming specifically. Four functions of the latter have to be of particular import to supers: career pathing, career guidance, fast-track programming, and executive-replacement planning. These functions are expected to be more seriously and effectively applied by supercorporations and given higher levels of funding and direction. The supers' experiments in manpower programming should put some of its functions deeply into the office of the chairman, with possibly precedent-breaking results.

11

A SUPERMANAGER'S INSIDE VIEW

LET US DRAW TOGETHER all that we have seen thus far about supercorporations' effects on the corporate life. We can try to project the views of one corporate man or woman, a sort of composite postindustrial manager, about his supercorporation and his own place in it. I have predicted that venture management will be one of the most vital and typical activities of the new supers. Therefore, this final chapter on the effects of supers on the business world and its people in part focuses on an outside manager's view of the venture management groups in his company. To complement this view, it also projects the probable opinions of a venture manager about the special role of the venture management function.

To begin with, our supermanager of the late 1980s works in a company that has "six different bosses"—that is, an office of the chairman—and deals with managers in other large corporations that also have this organizational structure at the top. His company and the others are committed to venture management as a principal means of accelerating growth. While he is not nearly as turned around in his working day as the members of the office of the chairman themselves, the manager finds that this structure is more than a public relations ploy. He finds that decisions come down the line faster and that more and faster recommendations or decisions are sometimes demanded (not awaited) from him or his immediate superior.

He and most of his associates feel that the quality of their performance has been brought up sharply by new requirements for much better homework. The difficulties he expected of getting six different orders from six different bosses rarely happen, for the members of the office of the chairman make the matter of speaking with one voice a way of life. That one voice, while flawed, is better scripted and faster in response and draws its authority and assurance more from knowledge and less from the power of command.

The two biggest changes are the way our composite manager is shaping up and liking it, and the way he is running his own shop. We can let him tell it in his own words:

"In the old days, there was a lot of talk about developing people, and there were some articles—partly fiction—about what the corporation was doing. The annual reports, in four colors, used to carry some commercials about this development work. There are not so many articles now, and the annual report is only half as long as it used to be. There is no way to measure the development of the people, except probably somehow in the bottom line, where the profits are much bigger. But if the outsider could see what I see, he would find that a lot of people have grown up in this corporation in the last few years. Some of them are going to be stars here."

The only thing harder to describe than the way our man and some of his colleagues are developing is the way they are managing their own areas. What seems to be making the difference in the corporation is that each manager down the line is picking up some of the changes himself. Again, let's let our manager speak for himself:

"There is a lot of talk about the firm being a growth company, and, in fact, the corporation has ground out some earnings per share that nobody thought possible. Then there is the talk about this company being a supercorporation. It really is growing faster than a lot of smaller ones, where growth is a lot easier. It sounds a little bit like the case studies in the advanced management seminar.

"Take the manpower plan, which started out like all the other programs that died off in about two years. I'm now developing people on the job, not just sending them to a couple of three-day courses. Now there is a better chance than at any time I can remember that I will have most of the people I need.

"In fact, when I look back, it isn't the same outfit at all, and one of the biggest changes is the one no one thought would happen—the corporation is actually living in some kind of management world, and so far the payoff is better than even the yes men would have said.''

Nevertheless, our supermanager, with ten years or more of corporate experience in a billion-dollar or larger enterprise, has developed a certain feeling about management programs that seems to combine numbness and cynicism. As he sees it, the cynicism is justifiable:

''Over the last ten years or more, all kinds of programs have been announced that have something to do with personnel. Performance bonuses have been in and out once or twice. There was a year or two when the corporate headquarters had a Ph.D. psychologist poking around, trying to make friends and doing some very private kind of counseling for a few managers. He was a little bit like an army chaplain. The office scuttlebutt actually had people believing that there were going to be some real chaplains on the payroll, but that never happened. That psychologist never seemed to get hooked up with the corporation, and he drifted back to his own practice.

''Also, every few years there was a big push on management development, or whatever it was called at the time. There were always some long reports saying how vital it was and how much benefit the corporation got—return on investment, they called it. Then a budget crunch or something came along, and headquarters staff assigned to the project disappeared. Some were fired, others went back to shuffling papers on some other project. I remember a few good management meetings and a lot of red tape and reports, but not much else—very little really—and the other people I know in what they call middle management can't put their fingers on much that lasted either.

''For a while I got pretty involved in performance-evaluation programs that later went nowhere and were eventually ignored. Some of the divisions broke their picks on management by objectives, but a few of them, including my own, seemed pretty happy with it for a couple of years. But now things are different, and for once, it just might last. Anyway, there are a lot fewer papers and a lot less conversation about 'human resource management.' It seems that most of the other managers and I now have a different kind of arrangement. It's hard to describe, because there aren't many buzz words and follow-up memos from above. Anyway, the bosses are getting more involved with their people—most of them, that is. Some will never change, and it begins to look as though some won't be given much more time in which to come around.

"Most of the higher level managers seem to be putting together the pieces of some of the old management programs, together with some newer things, too. For instance, some real communications are actually taking place. They aren't what they might be, of course, but they're much better than they were. Many of us managers feel that the top brass has at least some interest in us, because the bosses all along the line are keeping people a lot better posted on corporation matters and on their own personal prospects. Communications sound a lot less like government bulletins and more like real people.

"The top men—and we middle-level managers—don't pull punches and try to sugarcoat problems and failures as much. One of the big things, though, is our own company's TV network. They told us that companies like ours use more TV programming than the prime time on all the networks. Now, *that's* communications. Another big change is in what is being communicated. It is more than advance information on corporate PR releases, more than just the latest about who had a baby or took a vacation to Miami Beach or retired early.

"I know it's probably impossible to have a real team feeling with tens of thousands of employees and thousands of managers and supervisors and foremen. Still, many people have a greater feeling that they belong to something more than a bureaucracy, and some of them respond pretty well when they realize they are being treated as something more than numbers.

"Something else about our corporation in the last few years makes it almost a new place to work. Take the budgets, which are always such a drag. My opinions are being asked—it seems they're really wanted—on more than how to cut down on travel and telephone expenses. Quite a few managers, like me, are in on the plans for the whole profit center. We know more about what we are supposed to do and what our boss is doing. Our new picture of our own jobs really seems to tie in with this big planning operation. It's like the old management by objectives they used to preach, but it gets us managers a lot more involved in our own departments and groups.

"Now performance reviews make a little sense to us. We usually have to write up evaluations of ourselves, and you know the corporation still sometimes asks the impossible. Even so, quite a few of us managers have been beating our own targets, and there is a lot less hassling when we miss them.

"Some of the worst managers were put back into field sales or the factory, or out on the sidewalk. That never used to happen around here. There used to be men who were just putting in time for ten, twenty, thirty years. Some are still being protected, but more and more are making it on their own—or else. And that includes a lot more female managers than I ever thought I'd see. Most of the managers, including myself, are better off than ever. We can put in our two cents' worth, and we have more sensible jobs and requirements. We even get some help from above when we need it, instead of always getting hit with two more memos and a phone call.

"One of the places that has been in an uproar for years is the foreign business, which they now call the multinational business. There were times when it looked as though it would all go down the drain. There were some wild devaluations, a few new 'voluntary' import quotas, and more books full of new foreign regulations. The corporation lost some divisions in Latin America and Africa, and the Middle East has not been the same since about 1973. The corporation also decided to give up some contracts that were real money-makers, and sold parts of the foreign operations to companies with all kinds of strange names over there. It seemed to me that the corporation had lost just about everything in the International Division except Canada, and we had quite a battle there, too.

"The International Division did just about disappear in a couple of reorganizations, but the corporation is doing more business and making more money multinationally than in the good old days. There's a lot about corporate citizenship and the Third World that adds up. Somehow, the corporation can get its contracts and licenses and approvals more easily than it used to, and there have been hardly any expropriations or blowups since about 1983. A lot of foreigners—big ones, from the Far East, the Arab countries, all over—now hold stock in the corporation. Some people with wild names and faces took over big jobs here in the company and surprised a lot of people. They speak better English than we do, and they're usually pretty smart. A few were eased out quietly, but the rest of them have a home right here, in our corporation of all places.

"But the thing that's most unbelievable is the way our Americans are operating all over the world. Our divisions are not tied to just the United States any more, so that our Japanese and the EEC and other markets are handled right with what used to be our U.S. divisions. 'Multinational' is a word that makes sense, the way our corporation is wheeling and dealing now. None of us expected the amount of overseas traveling that goes on. But the big thing is that the different units can really put it all together into some kind of worldwide profit centers.

"Then," our manager adds, "there are those really big deals here at home that they are calling public-private partnerships, and some other big operations—'contract state' deals—where we actually are taking over some huge government research labs, and maybe some state's accounting and computer systems departments. Each one of these deals is bigger than some of our entire divisions were in the 1970s.

"And talk about dealing with your social problems. They're worse than ever now, and the 1970s seem like the good old days. The most I can say is that some of the predicted disasters didn't happen. Oregon cleaned up the Willamette River in the early 1970s, and a lot of other pollution is being beaten back in the same way. Our corporation has spent hundreds of millions of dollars on its pollution problems and still has had some pretty stiff lawsuits to fight. Anyway, after some stumbling, the company put together unbelievable reductions in its energy usage, and it also made good money on those contracts for training some tough characters in skilled trades. And some of them have moved up to foremen and some pretty good staff jobs—with an extra push here and there.

"You hear a lot more about alienation and the postindustrial society than you did ten or twelve years ago. The chairman seems to be spending most of his time in all kinds of outside conferences and citizens' committees, and spending a lot of company money on some far-out activities. He's also put one of our hourly employees, of all things, and a couple of different outsiders on our board—such as a student and some kind of a 'behaviorist.' We still don't have the tremendous worker representation on our board that they have had in Germany, Denmark, and Sweden since the late 1970s, and I doubt that we will.

"It's a very different business life, now that we're acting like some kind of a supercorporation—and yet, it's not completely different. The lower level employees have a lot more time off, and quite a choice in setting their own working hours. They also have shorter hours. But the other managers and I still haven't figured out how to do the job right, and do it between nine and five. There's always plenty of pressure—maybe more than ever—and lots of problems, but this corporation is a better place to work out the problems. The money is great (well, almost). I'm kidding about the 'almost.' Why I can see myself being financially independent by the time I'm about 50. But I'll bet I stay right here and let that money pile up higher. I'm far too involved in all this to step out just because I can afford to.''

An Outside Manager's View of Venture Management

An immediate, and sometimes downright unacceptable, change for our manager emits from that new venture management department. Other types of corporations, too, are doing more with venture-management-like arrangements of all types, but the supers are venturing with all the determination of ITT. Our manager, who is outside his corporation's venture management department, is probably envious of, and generally disturbed by, the unaccustomed freedom lavished on those in that obviously favored group. As he sees it:

"They're fiddling with all kinds of hush-hush projects, dealing directly with the heads of R&D, engineering, marketing, finance, and the other departments. Some of these hotshots are pretty young for all that top-level attention, and some of them are outsiders, brought in to fill fancy jobs that ought to have been filled by a good company man (like me).

"I just can't believe some of the things going on. My company started in grocery products; for all I know, it could be going into selling jewelry door to door. We also get announcements, company memos that aren't very informative, saying that the corporation has lent money to some little garage-size companies that nobody ever heard of, with product names that I can't pronounce.''

The manager will see all manner of strange goings-on. In time he will be surprised and grudgingly pleased that his corporation is now making quite a bit of money on one or two of those new ventures, but will wonder out loud whether the one or two that did hit will begin to repay the steep costs of the many more that flopped—the expensive pilot plant in Salem that was later sold for scrap, for instance, or the test marketing for months in Fort Wayne (or was it Columbus?) that soaked up all that TV money.

The first time a spin-off happens, the manager will be resentful. In his view, the corporation will be doing a disloyal and inhuman thing:

"Selling off the whole division! Everyone knows they had a lot of price cutting on their old products and they weren't making much money, but a lot of good, hard-working, loyal guys were really trying to turn that business around. Some of my friends in that division were with the company for more than twenty years, longer than I've been here, and the beginning of the division went back, maybe, to about 1900."

No corporate annual report will tie the two directly together, but the manager sees more and more of a relationship between this and many other divestments and plant closings and the unexpected increase in new products, new ventures, new profit centers, strange investments, multiple captives, and some acquisitions he thought the corporation would never have attempted.

On top of all this, he shares an opinion with most other managers that those characters in the venture management department have a better deal than anyone else:

"They seem to have a piece of the action, some sort of stock deal in their venture business, and nobody else has ever gotten anything like that out of the corporation—not even our group V.P. a couple of levels up the line. They do say that those fat cats in venture management don't get the regular raises and big bonuses that we other managers get, and maybe the venture guys don't get the company's fringe benefits, like the big group life coverage. Anyway, they have an unbelievable deal—those that stay. They do seem to have a higher turnover than the rest of us managers. Someone is always rocking the boat over there."

Venture Management As Seen from the Inside

To be sure, if our manager gets into the venture management group, he will be one of the few out of hundreds at his general level throughout the corporation. It looks different inside. As this venture manager might see it:

"The feeling here is more like a Vince Lombardi football team than the regular feeling of the corporate and divisional offices. But it's not exactly like a football team, either. It's really a lot like having your own business, but with a lot of backing and muscle from the top brass, and from a lot of outside people, too. Nobody in this department yet has left work early to get in a set of tennis or a round of golf before dark. Nobody even gets out on time, and there's really too much travel, too many working lunches; and we almost always carry home a bag of papers that must be looked at.

"Even so, not many people leave the venture management department voluntarily. One fellow got a fabulous offer from a sleepy old company. One or two others have been moved pretty fast into big positions right here in our company, and a few were just not up to the pace—or was it the entrepreneurial judgment they lacked? They got themselves transferred out with as little damage as possible to their careers, and so far most of them are still with the corporation in fairly good jobs. Over the life of our venture management department so far, most who left were riding the wrong horse, or were rated as having ridden it badly.

"The in-house announcements and the grapevine are both right: this is a higher risk business. We more than earn our extra bonuses and those small amounts of stock in our own ventures when we build them big. We get a lot of flak about it, but some of the middle managers who complain the loudest would never last in the venture management department."

To sum it up, the venturers know they have brought growth to their corporation that it never had before. The earnings of their ventures are still a minor part of the corporation's total earnings, but last year the ventures' increases in profits were over a quarter of the corporation's total increase in earnings per share. The venture management group is beginning to be recognized as one department that really produces, even though they will always get too much talk about some of their wild ideas that turn out to be losers.

Probably the most significant thing about the whole venture management department is their great team spirit and the way it sometimes seems to catch hold in some of the "old" departments and divisions:

"This corporation is really going somewhere now. It's beginning to be hard to remember the old grind of price wars, cyclical businesses that always seemed to be in the down phase, trying to sell me-too products, and spending time on hopeless little pet plans that never went anywhere. If anyone wants to see the business system working, he should look in here. And in another five years or so, even with a recession and some rough international problems, this so-called supercorporation will really be rolling.

"I've had some terrific offers from those executive recruiters, and a lot of other people around here have had those offers, too. Almost everyone is doing better here than he ever thought he would, and there are few other places that can come close to this kind of growth deal. Some people will probably get picked off, later, to take over a sick company or a turn-around situation, because of what they have built right here. When that happens, whoever goes will be doing all over again a lot of what this corporation has done.

"Most of us surviving managers, though, are going to stay right here. We finally have what we thought business was all about when we started. A few of us even think that we could end up running this whole $2 billion corporation, instead of those old-time managers who are running hard just to match their last year's profit in old-line businesses. Yes, it's quite a setup, and one that we managers would not have believed even six or seven years ago."

The supercorporation managers whose thoughts we have just tapped are likely composites of today's better managers as they will evolve in the postindustrial world of the supers. They will find many of the same old problems in the 1980s, plus some nasty new ones, foreign and domestic. The solutions that these managers create will work, partly. The far tougher foreign and domestic competition will have bent or broken some managers and companies, and will have been the making of others—the supers and their new breed of supermanagers.

PART THREE

SUPERCORPORATIONS
in
OUR WORLD

*We are all Indians. . . . We live as the Indians
. . . lived, between cultures, compelled to re-
adjust ourselves to forces that will not wait
for us.*

—BRUCE CATTON

Our whole way of life has been destroyed by progress. As our familiar world slips by, we find ourselves churning in alternatives.
Our postindustrial society will be even more wealthy, prone to
change, and socially restive than the one that laid to rest our hap-
pier days.

Within this new society, we can expect the supercorporation to
be a prime mover. Its energy will lap into nonbusiness spheres, for
better or for worse. We "Indians" now have early warning—to
program our responses to the new supercorporations and to shape
the supers as part of a world in which our migrant spirits may find
moorings.

The Sociocorporate Interface

Part One reviewed the early but mounting evidence for the evolution of the supercorporation. Part Two examined some of the ways in which the emerging supers may make corporate life a new—and possibly better—ball game. Here and there, in a few of the large conventional corporations, bureaucracy is already losing its grip. New fields of enterprise, new management concepts, new financing methods, and new aggressiveness are pumping real growth into what used to be stolid mass. This is only a foretaste of what full-fledged supercorporations will be doing to reach that exclusive status.

The supers, oversized and overachieving, are likely to have as great an influence on the social perils of the postindustrial society as I have predicted they will have on the business world and its people. Part Three looks into the future to see how supercorporations may affect the world beyond the corporation and gives insights into some of the attainable benefits of supers—if they are on their best behavior.

Our first subject is the ultimate good and evil potentialities of supercorporations. Next we will consider the head-on conflict between those who abhor any social contributions by profit-making companies and those who insist on such contributions. Then we will cross-check four huge sociocorporate movements against the characteristics of the supercorporation. These movements are the establishment of more public-private partnerships, the evolution of the contract state, the involvement of U.S. corporations in less developed countries, and the raising of new cities. Not surprisingly, we will see that the supercorporation has unique capabilities for advancing these sociocorporate movements.

Before attacking this agenda, let us tick off the possible values of Part Three for a variety of readers. Outside directors and others working at the top of the largest corporations will find a rarely presented perspective of what these corporations should or should not be doing about a society that is in pieces. Corporate managers, planners, and specialists can review four quite new areas for expansion, each of which has larger potential than many of the other fields available to them. Medium-size and smaller companies may glimpse pieces of these areas suitable for their own growth.

Also, workers and students of foreign aid may be cheered, amid deep gloom in their fields, by new opportunities to be brought by supercorporations. The multitude of professional and business service people can look at some of the fields that supers, semisupers, and their emulators are expected to handle in new ways. People in both manufacturing and services may want to make some preparations to serve and benefit from these new directions in large postindustrial corporate enterprises.

Legislators, government executives, public technicians, regulators, academics, and social critics will be exposed to the several social possibilities of supercorporations at the same time as are the corporate executives themselves. They will have reactions to this panorama of supers in society, and they may wish to make early inputs in order to mold the supers for what they consider the general welfare.

Most of all, the *individual,* the one who does the work and pays the taxes—that is, most of us—can clearly grasp the outlook for supercorporations and their possibilities for helping or harming us all. We will be watching two interlocking expressions of the supercorporation: the pure super, which meets our four requirements for admission to the club, and the much more numerous semisuper, and other emulators, which will take on much of the coloration and importance of the true super.

12

THE BASIC INCLINATION

THIS CHAPTER takes on the first two tasks of Part Three: a consideration of the ultimate good or evil of supercorporations and the debate as to whether profit-making companies should even attempt to make social contributions.

Supercorporations—Good or Evil?

This is not necessarily an optimistic book. On the contrary, it clearly recognizes that the future will be bleak and violent if supercorporations should veer toward their worst side and multiply the repeated wrongs that have been done in the name of business or free enterprise.

We know much of this worst side. Business has too often been callous toward consumers. Remember those hundreds of faulty school buses? There was organized lawlessness in the great aircraft brake caper, with manufacturer-planned deceptions on the capability of its brakes to stop a new fighter plane. Add the conspiracy of an auto manufacturer's employees to falsify the test results of the cars' pollution emissions. That company paid a fine of $7 million.

Corporations have also engaged in excessive lobbying. Who will forget Dita Beard and her cronies? In the Watergate scandal, too many big corporate executives improperly financed the people who gave us the "plumbers," "dirty tricks," and all the rest.

Too, big business has been guilty of sheer ineptitude, with its disastrous effects on the victimized employees and stockholders and their families, on suppliers—even on whole communities. There was the case of Anaconda, once the world's largest copper company, which managed the trip from traditional blue-chip status to a loss of $356 million and 3,000 jobs. Not to mention the defense contractor, which spun out of control and posted a $400 million loss in just one year. And remember the salad oil deal? Though cooked up by a clever swindler, it was made possible by the unwitting support of long-established and well-regarded banks and stockbrokerage houses, among others.

Books are filled with these and other reports from the dark side of corporate doings. The argument here is not that government and other institutions are inherently more ethical or effective. But if supercorporations are only going to magnify the faults and frauds of conventional corporations and the swinging conglomerates, we should seek to crush them in their cocoons, before they emerge with extreme power and fasten themselves onto the back of our society.

This pessimistic option is one of the chief reasons this book exists. There is a chance that some supercorporations may run amok among us, as ITT has done. Few people in our society can afford not to heed this early warning, and we should all focus our sights on the supercorporations as they come up over the horizon.

This early warning could yield an abiding concern, followed by private and public checkmating of any new depredations by supercorporations, semisupers, and other emulators. This possible sequence of concern leads to the guardedly optimistic face of this book. Rather than burying ourselves in criminal law, trust-busting and the like, I believe we should also explore the quantum opportunities for social improvement that are peculiarly inherent in the supercorporations of the later 1970s and the 1980s.

Our mental screens are already glutted with visions of the bad influences that today's large corporations have had on our society. We now need to open our minds to some fresh possibilities for change. At the very least, we should consider the reverse—that is, how our society may break through the typical corporate shell of inertia and exert influence for the good. If nothing else, society will continue placing legal and ethical restraints on corporate excesses—pollution, firings of 30-year employees without a pension, dangerous products, shoddy services, and the like. But this societal pressure on the large corporation, by itself, would mop up only some of the excesses, some of the time.

A more positive societal force may be exerted through the people who work in the corporations themselves. Though it is usually overlooked, the possibility exists that corporate executives and employees may in the future have higher social and business standards and may accordingly alter corporate performance from within.

A second beneficial force on the large corporation—one to be described in detail later in the book—may result from the vast opportunities to make a lot of money by exploiting large new markets. These markets, such as the creation and operation of entire new cities, happen to promise some desirable social effects, but they will also stand on their own in the usual sense of profit taking.

These two forces of the postindustrial society may forge a change for the better in the quality of at least a few large corporations. This controversial thought of redemption reinforces the internal movements within the business community that we saw are creating the supercorporations.

Perhaps two examples of contemporary conventional corporate performance will help suggest the better possibilities that may be coaxed out of the supercorporations. In an earlier time the company-owned town was one of the most unappetizing artifacts of big companies. Since then, many such towns have been abandoned or converted into more typical communities. U.S. Steel seems to have gone above and beyond the call of duty in its former Gary, West Virginia, company coal town. U.S. Steel refurbished the old company houses, repaved the streets, built new utilities, and contributed cash and equipment to get the 3,000-member town started as a going, independent city. That was in 1971. In 1973 the mayor of Gary wrote me that U.S. Steel had done its job well, and that he felt his fellow townspeople were glad they were able to make this transition; now they feel they are masters of their own destiny.

A second example of some better corporate citizenship today is more general: the possibly novel thought of the corporation as a patron of the arts. I suspect that U.S. business and businessmen collectively are quantitatively history's largest art patrons, overshadowing the legendary Medici and all others. Qualitatively, you will get some passionately differing opinions, with some pointing to ugly buildings and others to great art collections. Somewhere in between is the Cummins Engine Company and the Miller family of Columbus, Indiana, which has made possible more top-quality architecture in that town of 27,000 people than can be found in similar towns almost anywhere else. Columbus is not a company town in the old-fashioned sense, and the Millers did not order the fire department and others to commission outstanding designs. They just offered to pay the sizable extra costs of retaining the country's leading architects—and it worked.

With this attempt to balance today's corporate crimes and contributions, let us consider further whether and how tomorrow's supers may be inclined toward their best potentials.

Should Corporations Invest in Social Problems?

Our conditional optimism shows that supercorporations and their followers *could* perhaps do something constructive for our world. The next question is whether they *should* do so, if they can. Before you answer yes, consider that this question has been raised seriously and with great force by such observers as Dr. Milton Friedman. Dr. Friedman, professor of economics at the University of Chicago, is on record as stating categorically that profit-making corporations should under no circumstances invest corporate resources in socially oriented activities that return a lower than normal profit or no profit at all.

Dr. Friedman's position included two major points. First, a corporation wrongly arrogates to itself the decision as to what are the most socially desirable activities to support. These decisions merely reflect, Dr. Friedman says, the clichés that happen to be current among intellectuals at the moment.

His second objection to corporate social investments is that a corporation, which has no money of its own, must spend the money of stockholders, customers, or employees. Dr. Friedman declares that it is highly inappropriate for a corporation to spend someone else's money for social programs or for anything else that does not optimize directly the profits of the corporation.

In a letter to me, Dr. Friedman wrote that he would make his arguments even more strongly against corporation spending on social programs:

First, I would point out, in connection with the problem of how one knows what is socially desirable, the striking example of the German businesses in pre-Nazi Germany that supported Hitler on the ground that it was socially desirable to have stability and a strong government. They were exercising their social responsibility precisely along the lines that people urge U.S. corporations to exercise it.

Second, I would stress more strongly, insofar as there is competition, no corporation has any leeway in exercising social responsibility. The mom and pop corner grocery store obviously cannot exercise a social responsibility except insofar as the proprietors spend their own money by accepting a smaller return than they otherwise could attain. A corporation can exercise social responsibility in the sense in which it has some meaning if and only if it has some monopoly power either on the side of the sale of its product or on the hiring of factors of production. In the first case, it exercises its social responsibility at the expense of either stockholders or customers; in the second place, at the expense of its employees. Hence I would now have stated more explicitly that any speech by any corporate executive in which he boasts that the corporation has been exercising its social responsibility should be a *prima facie* evidence of violation of the Anti-Trust Act and should immediately bring Justice Department prosecution of his concern for violation of monopoly powers.[1]

Aside from my respectful but deep disagreement with Dr. Friedman's viewpoint, there appears in 1974 little prospect of corporations reversing their engines and following Dr. Friedman's recommendations. The amounts of cash and other resources spent on social concerns have increased, net of the puffery that overstates them.

There are few measurements of the size and upward trend of corporate social undertakings, but the following comments hint at the way the tide is running. The Committee for Economic Development has stated: ". . . The public wants business to contribute a good deal more to the goals of a good society. Its expectations of business have been broadened . . . to include becoming more broadly involved in activity improving the social environment."[2]

John R. Bunting, chairman and chief executive officer of the First Pennsylvania Corporation and First Pennsylvania Bank, comments:

We view these two considerations, profits and social responsibility, so often portrayed as "either/or," as anything but mutually exclusive. The

[1] Used with permission of the author.
[2] "Social Responsibilities of Business Corporations," Research and Policy Committee, Committee for Economic Development, June 1970.

much-touted corporate social responsibility that refers to business's involvement in social issues is now popularly said to have a healthy and favorable effect on corporate profitability in the long run.

. . . we also see the positive results of such policies in a context which is more immediate. And we think our operating results authenticate this belief.[3]

The business community of the early and middle 1970s is clearly with the Committee for Economic Development and Mr. Bunting, not with Dr. Friedman. In fact, one of the few certainties for the future of large corporations is that the size of their social undertakings will increase.

To recap, the ever larger corporation of tomorrow, especially the supercorporation, could inflict extreme damage on our domestic and world society. One of the main purposes of this book is to give loud early warning of this possibility. Alternatively, we may find that our society will change the large corporation, by legal, individual, and new profit-making forces.

Internal forces in the business community are already leading to the creation of supercorporations, and the possibility that these and other large corporations may evolve a different nature is the basis for some optimism. The supers and their imitators may become the engines for powering order-of-magnitude changes in the infrastructure of U.S. and world society. The direction they will follow will be decided partly by the readers of this book through their influence on the new supercorporations.

Although it is debatable whether profit-making corporations ought to invest in socially oriented activities that produce less profit than these corporations would ordinarily require of their ventures, the general opinion of the business community is that they should, and the fact is that they are doing so with increasing frequency.

[3] John L. Paluszek, "Organizing for Corporate Social Responsibility," *AMA Special Study No. 51* (Winter 1972–1973), p. 11.

13

SUPERCORPORATIONS in PUBLIC-PRIVATE PARTNERSHIPS

OUR POSTINDUSTRIAL CORPORATIONS, especially the supercorporations, will thrive on a number of kinds of ventures. Public-private partnerships are an important example.

Let us start with definitions, acknowledging some unavoidable overlap between public-private partnerships and business ventures in the contract state, a category to be discussed later.

Public-private partnerships are businesslike corporations that (1) are permitted to make a profit, (2) perform some specific function desired by government, and (3) are operated in close cooperation with government functions. The Federal National Mortgage Association and the Communications Satellite Corporation are two cases in point.

By contrast, in business ventures in the contract state (as discussed in the next chapter), the business entity takes over all or nearly all of the specified functions from the government. In contracting, the government merely chooses a contractor, pays a fee, oversees the performance of its contract, and does little else. An example of a business venture in the contract state was the entire running of one public school in Gary, Indiana, by a private, profit-making corporation.

Regarding public-private partnerships, it will be useful to distinguish them from the longer established governmental corporations such as the TVA and the Port Authority of New York & New Jersey.

The latter are totally different corporate forms for accomplishing assigned public purposes. Such governmental corporations (1) are totally government-owned, not partially owned by individual stockholders such as you or me; (2) are not operated for profit, whereas the public-private partnerships are operated for quite large profits; (3) are largely manned by civil service employees and have most of the other paraphernalia of government units, whereas the public-private corporations look and act much more like business enterprises; and (4) have been in operation for as long as about 40 years, whereas public-private corporations have become significant only within the last dozen years.

I will first describe public-private partnerships and then venture an educated guess as to the effects of supercorporations on them.

Public-Private Partnerships in Profile

It took a public-private partnership, sponsored by President John F. Kennedy and passed by the Congress of the United States, to bring you the Communications Satellite Corporation (Comsat)—and near-perfect television reception from any place on the globe. President Richard M. Nixon's 1972 tour of the Great Wall of China, in living color, was seen instantly from Honolulu to Old Mission, Michigan, partly because the U.S. government made a business deal with AT&T and other conventional companies. The government's part of the bargain was to provide what it could do easily—put the needed communications satellites into earth orbit. AT&T and the other businesses provided what they could do easily—operate the communications networks fed by the orbiting satellites. This public-private partnership has done what any good partnership should do: it has rendered a far better result than its partners could have produced separately.

It is instructive to see that the public-private Comsat has the full array of corporate characteristics. It has over 100,000 individual stockholders, and originally had some 90 communications carriers also as stockholders. Its stock is listed on the New York, Midwest, and Pacific Coast stock exchanges. The company has registrars, transfer agents, inside and outside directors, and an annual audit by its public accounting firm. It also has audits by the Internal Revenue Service. After one of them, IRS collected $2.7 million in additional taxes for the years 1967 through 1970.

Comsat buys its satellite launching services from the National Aeronautics and Space Administration and pays for these services at their calculated costs.

This public-private partnership has been a success by any measure. It has done its assigned job of providing satellite services on a business basis, in harness with its partial owners, some of the telephone companies in the United States. It upgrades its services as any good profit-maker should; the fourth generation of its satellites has been fired into geostatic orbit 22,300 miles above the equator. Comsat has also entre-preneurially sought to broaden its business base through new services. One is substituting its communications services for the established ship-to-shore communications; Comsat has signed up the U.S. Navy for a $28 million contract. Unlike the government agencies that have been manipulated by those they are supposed to control, Comsat is seeking to replace its own largest stockholder, AT&T, in the cable business.

After 11 years of existence, Comsat in 1973 earned $36.3 million. Although technically classified as a utility, Comsat would rank 221 in profits in 1973 among the 500 largest industrials.

The Federal National Mortgage Association, popularly called Fannie Mae, is quite a different offspring of public-private partnership, and another instructive venture in its field. Rather than being created out of whole cloth, as was Comsat, Fannie Mae spent the first 31 years of its life as a government agency. It was started in 1938 under President Franklin D. Roosevelt, with the purpose of assisting in the financing of home mortgages.

By 1968, Fannie Mae had become a business with gross revenues of $408 million and pretax net income of $20.5 million, maintaining a secondary market in FHA and VA mortgages. This market is essential in moderating the peaks and valleys in mortgage financing. Fannie Mae was originally capitalized with preferred stock worth $160 million, held by the U.S. secretary of the treasury, and common stock worth $140 million, owned by participating financial institutions.

Then, in 1968, the public-private status of Fannie Mae took form: the corporation sold debentures in the securities market and used the proceeds to buy out all the federal government's preferred stock. Fannie Mae thereby became privately owned, but is still a public-private partnership. Among its public aspects, in addition to its basic dealings in government-backed mortgages, are the regulatory authority of the

U.S. secretary of Housing and Urban Development (in, among other areas, the setting of the debt limit and the ratio of debt to equity) and the appointment of five of its fifteen directors by the President of the United States. Also, the secretary of Housing and Urban Development may require that a portion of Fannie Mae's mortgage purchases be related to the national purpose of providing adequate housing for low- and moderate-income families, with a reasonable economic return to the corporation.

Here, then, is a second public-private partnership dedicated to a second social concern. It, too, is growing and prospering in its own organizational version of the still experimental phenomenon of public-private ownership.

With two rousing wins, we turn to a third effort that had difficulty getting off the ground at its scheduled speed. This effort is at the state level of government and consists of still a different structure for attacking another group of social concerns, urban renewal, including housing construction.

New York State's Urban Development Corporation is one of the most advanced of all government agencies seeking to solve specific social problems, and UDC relies heavily on private-sector corporate partners. UDC has extraordinary powers to acquire land, set aside local zoning, work around local building codes, and otherwise cut months and years from the process of urban renewal. One of its key powers is the setting up of partnerships with business corporations to build, own, and operate its development projects. The terms and profits UDC offers its private partners are good; some say outstandingly so.

With its panoply of extraordinary authority, large funding, strong management, and the means to attract heavy participation from private partners, UDC has recently set records in the amount of redevelopment achieved and in its speed of performance. Still, on occasion, even UDC has been delayed by a lack of needed private partners—with attendant delays in solving problems and in realizing profits that could have been earned by the needed private partners.

Unfortunately, we cannot expect most conventional government agencies to achieve the same outstanding performance as UDC. We can expect that still more agencies will be added to those now struggling with urban redevelopment and most other attempted social solutions. We as citizens will need insightful, flexible, smart private partners doubly for the typical government agencies, and will continue to need such partners for the rare public partners such as UDC. Although the private partners of UDC and other similar organizations are not yet supercorporations, there is a good chance that the special characteristics of supercorporations will enable them to attain some of their growth by capturing large amounts of the public-private partnership potential for the ultimate benefit of all.

Supercorporations as Private Partners

Enter the supercorporations? Perhaps so. Comsat succeeded in part because of the ability of AT&T and others to participate. While not a supercorporation in our terms, AT&T, with 1972 total assets of $67.1 billion and over 775,000 employees, was abundantly large enough to be a partner in the new venture and still continue its basic businesses. Note thoroughly the two requirements: the private-sector partners have to be big and smart enough to participate sufficiently to help the new partnership succeed, and to be able, simultaneously, to continue to increase their established businesses.

We have suggested that both size and uncommon flexibility to diversify are needed for the private-sector corporations that would consummate a partnership with governments in large new social enterprises. If we accept the size and diversity criteria, the next question is: Where does our much-troubled society find large, flexible business partners? Not necessarily in those conventional big corporations that are having trouble keeping their heads above water in their own markets. Also, not necessarily in those 1960 conglomerates that have had problems staying in the black—or staying in one piece.

We have led ourselves back to the supercorporation. We know that it will be a strongly financed large company whose management has not gone to seed, an organization that has already moved some of its tens of thousands of employees to break the old molds. It will be, for example, a company motivated to get out of passé businesses, to switch from a retailing base into manufacturing, multiple financial services, and real estate development, and to do this with 13 consecutive years of growth in sales, earnings, and earnings per share. We are not saying that Sears, Roebuck ought to start work on an Indian reservation in upstate New York. We are saying that the same rare talents that can help establish supercorporation status are some of the most natural talents for making successful the future public-private partnerships needed to help meet our postindustrial social concerns and rebuild the pieces of our society.

The few public-private partnerships that are already attacking successfully a handful of our social concerns have exhibited a unique power to unite the strengths of government and profit-making private enterprise. In two inordinately successful examples, Communications Satellite Corporation and the Federal National Mortgage Association, the public-private partnership has accomplished vastly more than any partner could have done on its own. The partnerships to date have necessarily been founded without the supercorporations, which have not yet arrived in the business world. The requirements for the private partners in future public-private partnerships in projects of social concern will demand the noted capabilities of supercorporations, semisupers, and other unusually large and capable corporations approaching super status. Some authorized social projects are already lagging because of a dearth of appropriate partners, and still more could suffer without the advent of supercorporations.

14

SUPERCORPORATIONS and the CONTRACT STATE

LET US TRY OUR FORESIGHT with another of my futurist ideas, that of the contract state. We will speculate on how supercorporations may fit into this potentially huge vehicle for coping with some of the social perils of the postindustrial society.

Although we have a book of evidence of the coming of the super-corporation, any big growth of the contract state is today only a possibility. The contract state is so new relative to social concerns that most of you will rightly ask for more background.

In the phrase "contract state," "state" refers to a nation or other unit of government; "contract" refers to the practice of farming out government services to businesses that agree to render those services for a profit.

With some long-standing exceptions, widespread state contracting does not exist anywhere today. This chapter explores the odds for and against the contract state being vigorously expanded. You will recall that the time span of this futurist book is the later 1970s and the 1980s. However, the full flowering of the contract state might come after 1990.

Several examples of contract services will set the stage. Most types of governmental units, from national to local, have hired contractors to handle the construction of public office buildings, dams, airports, sewers, schools, barracks, government-owned utilities, and dozens of other similar projects. In addition, governmental units have almost always contracted for telephone services, most weapons and military supplies, and advertising, including multi-million-dollar armed services recruiting campaigns. All this is so common that we take it for granted.

It is equally taken for granted that the various governments will provide their own educational, police, fire-fighting, mail, and similar services to the tune of $200 billion annually. These services represent the "make" side of make-versus-buy decisions. With all the other revolutions and switches going on, there has somehow been almost no movement in the time-encrusted make-versus-buy decisions of governments.

A recent exception has been the contracting of pieces of the process of elementary education to profit-making companies. This total reversal from make to buy is controversial, and the results are not yet promising. These arrangements are, nonetheless, an example of the kinds of contracts that would be made in a contract state.

The question we are discussing is whether the farming out of one school in the ghetto of Gary, Indiana, is a one-time lapse from the centuries-old tradition of publicly made education, or whether our whole concept of the nature of government services is going to be turned upside down by beginnings such as this one. Will many of the schools, hospitals, and welfare departments, the mails, the geodetic survey, customs, the census, and so on be provided by contract, as is the construction of post offices, highways, and missile launching pads?

The concept of the contract state stretches over so much territory that it will be useful to eliminate a number of things that it does not encompass.

The contract state is not the same as the public-private partnerships portrayed in the previous chapter. The difference is that the contracts in the contract state would provide for most or all of the specified service to be performed by the business contractor. For example, the Department of Defense does little to aid AT&T in providing the telephone services for the North American Air Defense Command in Colorado Springs. In contrast, the government does much to facilitate the operation of public-private partnerships. In housing and other urban developments, the government partner condemns land and conveys it on an advantageous basis to the private partner. Without the government partner's input, the intended result might be unattainable. To state the difference in another way, contracts in the contract state put all or much of the job in the hands of the business contractor. Public-private partnerships make the public partner an active one, often crucially so.

Neither does the contract state involve government financing or subsidizing of businesses. We already have financing for mink farmers, a loan guarantee for Lockheed Aircraft Corp., and subsidies for shipbuilders—none of which sounds at all like the contract state as presented here.

The contract state is the opposite of governmental operation of businesses usually run by private enterprise—for instance, rope walks, printing shops, and retail stores (in the post exchanges and ships' stores).

The contract state, further, has nothing to do with the many governmental interventions in, or services for, the business world, such as industrial development corporations, sponsored cooperatives, and "Buy American" acts.

With the contract state thus defined and delimited, we are less concerned with whether the contract state should come into full being and more concerned with whether supercorporations will actually expand the currently stable dimensions of contracting for the state.

I predict a multi-billion-dollar increase in state contracting, without knowing how many billions "multi" will become. Nevertheless, only the merest multi-billion-dollar increase in contracting would afford bonanzas that are scarcely on the shopping lists of today's corporate planners.

To size up this approaching multi-billion-dollar transition in the way we are governed and served, it will be helpful to see how the character of the coming supercorporations would affect the nature of the contract state. Little has been written as yet on this potentially enormous subject, but first let us note the advantages and disadvantages for the citizenry of the contract state.

Advantages of the Contract State

The advantages of the contract state, to nearly everyone except the bureaucrats who will lose their jobs, are extensive.

EFFICIENCY AND EFFECTIVENESS

The obvious first advantage of business corporations handling a much larger number of services under contract to the government is the probability of greater economic and social efficiency and effectiveness. For example, in 1970 New York City found that it cost its department of sanitation $50 per ton to handle garbage. The same service, performed by private businesses, cost $18 per ton, 36 percent of the cost to the city. The private operators also paid income and other taxes and made a profit on the $18 per ton price.

These "obvious" improvements are not based upon a meat-axe slashing of approved services. The opportunity for enhancement of the values added lies in the differences between the public and private systems for rendering services. "Give it to the government, and crime won't pay" is a widely shared feeling, but one that does not always reflect the facts. Evidences of business inefficiency range from confused charge accounts to the questioned quality of steel plates in U.S. Navy submarines to the reliability of home appliances. There are, on the other hand, occasional instances of sustained good performance by government bureaus. The Processed Products Inspection Service of the U.S. Department of Agriculture, which has been solely supported for over 40 years by its own fee earnings, is a case in point.

When business is more efficient than government, more than the profit motive and the business tradition separate the private performance of a business service in the contract state from a governmental unit's performance of the same service under the same general conditions. The governmental system of escalating appropriations with little review of effectiveness or efficiency is too well known. A less recognized flaw on the government side is the tendency of bureaus to distort or disregard the original intent of their legislative directives. In testifying before the U.S. Senate Subcommittee on Executive Reorganization in 1968, I scored the lack of a searching review by the legislative branch of the executive departments' use of funds. Every senator present agreed fully, but after more than six years, there is still no review system, and government departments still wander largely where they will.

As soon, however, as a profit-making company enters the picture, the rules of the game change. The bidding and contracting procedure, though imperfect, is often open. The statement of what the contractor is to do is verifiable and has many pages of contractual safeguards for the government. Cancellation procedures are established, should the contractor's performance or the government's situation warrant termination of the project. A good deal is disclosed along the way, and all three branches of government have the power to investigate or judge any and every aspect of the contract and its execution. Also, unsuccessful bidders may attack the contract award or the contractor's performance. This has been done successfully in federal government awards of contracts for computers, consulting services, and building construction, among others.

The crux of the matter is that the contracting system, in its imperfect practice, can usually be made better (that is, less worse) than the government's own performance. The contracting system contains the seeds of its own betterment, if and when the public wants it to work better. In sorry contrast, few if any politicians or government administrators have found a means for improving the government's level of efficiency and effectiveness, regardless of the social pressure for improvement.

The contracting for new forms of educational services is a more enlightening case than has been perceived. Even if all the contracts miss their targets, the contracting system will outshine its government counterpart. The contracting system enabled boards of education, the Department of Health, Education and Welfare, and many others to set desired goals, try to meet them with radically new services, evaluate performance, and take corrective action. The relatively few millions thus allocated to innovate educational experiments taught us all something about the opportunities and limitations in educating disadvantaged youngsters—the limitations thus far overwhelm the opportunities. The awful contrast with the billions wasted in public schools gives us an inkling of the practical difference between contracting performance and government performance. This comparison is much more involved, but the basic point remains: contracting has a systemic advantage over government's in-house performance.

QUALITATIVE DIFFERENCES

In the contracting system, two kinds of competition can call forth qualitative differences in the performance of public tasks. One is competition between contractors; the other is competition among governments and government officials. Take graphic arts as an example.

Governments are among the largest buyers of printing, and some governmental units are themselves large printers. Governments have every reason to improve the *quality* of the graphic arts processes, and not just to get tight bids on printing jobs or printing presses.

Governments spend some tens of millions of dollars every year merely for routine administration, including bidding, negotiating, auditing, and other procedures in printing purchases. Now, say that some of this money were allocated to contracting with businesses to obtain specific qualitative improvements in the value received from the hundreds of millions now spent on printing. Such investments, hypothetically, could result in new ways of integrating computers with the printing process, leading to greater accuracy and more current issuance of government materials, at the same or lower costs. The money and the normal motivations of the society would be used as leverage for doing the accepted jobs better. The contracts administrator would not feel pressured to be an inventor. Also, the all too rare sources of qualitative improvement would not be crushed by devoting every administrative dollar to beating down the prices for the same old things. Both tough bid competition and qualitative improvements can come, sometimes, in the contract state. Costs would go down, efficiency would go up, and qualitative improvements would be more often fostered than suppressed. This example expresses the tone, as well as the process, of the corporate state.

Another qualitative advantage in performance contracting would be the unwinding of one of the worst snarls of government bureaucracy at all levels, the extreme incentive for empire building. Some say that government employees do not have incentives to perform. This is false. Government employees have a high incentive to perform, but they usually measure improvement in their performance by increases in the number, and often the ratings and salaries, of the employees in their group.

This is an outrageously bad incentive, but oh, how it works. I have burned the midnight oil with top committees of the Chamber of Commerce of the United States trying to crack this problem. So have uncounted legislative committees, efficiency experts, and irate taxpayers. The system whips us all every time—to the extent that not even a theoretical remedy has been generally accepted.

Enter the contract state, and for the first time there is a basis for using government incentive pay differently. With tens or hundreds of thousands of government employees going out of style because of the contract state, the remaining bureaucrats can finally be made to accept another basis for incentive compensation. In fact, they should be the first to detect a need for a new incentive basis. Initially, that basis can be the phasing out—instead of the agglomerating—of the unneeded hordes of bureaucrats. Longer term, the incentive basis would be the performance achieved by the remaining government administrators, as measured by their contractors' performance relative to the legislative or executive performance goals. This sounds millennial, but it is one of the few rays of light since bureaucracies began.

INDUSTRY-GOVERNMENT COMPETITION

Knowing that some businesses get fat and lazy, and occasionally collusive, the contract state would not depend entirely on typical business competition for the improved performance of government services. There would remain in government a sizable corps of contracting officers and employees. With their incentive compensation system geared to their contractors' performance, they would wield a strong club against bad performance. And, wherever possible, the government contracting officers and staffs would also have the right to go back to "making" their services instead of buying them.

Other forms of government-industry competition could properly be used to help keep contractors and potential contractors productive. Competition among various units and levels of government would be salutary. If some states contracted out the operation of their employment agencies, while others did not, both groups of states could be motivated to improve because of the new competition thus set in motion.

Disadvantages of the Contract State

The disadvantages of the contract state are impressive. We will also see that supercorporations will, unfortunately, add to some of these disadvantages.

INEFFICIENCY—AND WORSE

In addition to philosophical and political disadvantages, a practical disadvantage of the contract state may be inefficiency of the contractors, perhaps compounded by too-cozy relationships with the governments' contracting personnel.

As to inefficiency, we have already acknowledged that businesses are not immune. The most inefficient businesses might prove to be no better than the inefficient government bureaus they would replace.

Contracts would have to be offered for long enough periods to entice bidders. The lengthy contract periods might allow time for all manner of inefficiencies to creep in, with the government unable to use its remedies for periods of months or years.

INAPPROPRIATENESS

Many would argue that the contracting of certain humane services, such as welfare, would degrade these services even further in terms of impersonality and ineffectiveness. Such contracted services would presumably be carried on at the expense of those members of society least able to defend themselves. The contract state might simply not fit some of the recognized needs of disadvantaged citizens.

POLITICS AS USUAL

Another practical disadvantage of the contract state may be that government services would not be any freer of politics than is the case today. Aside from the inefficiencies that would be thus continued, the political games could either cancel the advantages of the contract state or bring new problems that would not otherwise exist today—or both.

The range of political possibilities is wide, signaling that the politics of government services might be replaced by the equally bad politics of the contracting game in the contract state. As the French proverb says it, plus ça change, plus c'est la même chose: "the more things change, the more they remain the same."

LABOR PROBLEMS

A decision on the part of organized labor, or unorganized labor, against the contract state as a matter of principle could override all advantages of this system. There is no obvious basis for such a decision, but the chance of it must be considered as a potential disadvantage.

Another potential disadvantage is that organized labor might replace collective bargaining, in contracting situations, with pressure on the legislative and executive branches. This would remove contract awards still further from productivity than is now our experience in the accustomed contracting fields. Or, if contracting leads to fewer and larger economic units, the society may become even more vulnerable than it now is to nationwide work stoppages—authorized or wildcat—and sick-outs. Other labor disadvantages face the corporate state, but these will make the point.

It must be added that some labor leaders would view all these labor-fed disadvantages as advantages of the contract state.

LOSS OF COMMUNITY INTEREST

Uncounted hours are donated by individuals to some of the services, such as hospitals and libraries, that might be let out to profit-making corporations in the contract state. The retired career woman who rides a school bus in order to get to her volunteer work in a school library might lose interest if she felt she were giving her time to a large profit-making corporation, the stock of which she could not afford to buy. Thus, these volunteer hours might be greatly reduced in the contract state.

TOTALITARIAN TENDENCIES

Some would hold that the order-of-magnitude reduction in the number of people directly employed by government would make both government and contractors more responsive to the people.

Others would claim that there could be totalitarian tendencies, even unintentionally, in the contract state. In one direction there could be close relationships between government contracting officers and the contractors. They could bypass both the legislative and the executive branches at all levels, enrich the contractors in both money and power, and build not a contract state but a syndicate state, responsive to hardly anyone. In another direction, the business community, greatly enlarged by the contract state, might use its augmented wealth and strength to increase its influence on elections, thus subverting representative government. In a third direction, the degree of concentration of economic power might be further increased. The number of large companies made larger by huge contracts might more than offset the gains that small businesses would realize from their awards of contracts for small services.

Supercorporate Impact

This is not the place to debate whether the contract state should be adopted. It is a good idea, however, to speculate further on whether the supercorporation is likely to advance or retard a movement toward the contract state. The probable answer is that supers will come down more heavily on the advantage side of the corporate state, and therefore can be expected to give some otherwise unavailable support to the contract state movement.

Supercorporations will be organically suited to pick off more than their share of business in the contract state. Economists have usually thought that large scale does not automatically bring the greatest economic efficiency. However, the potentially greater ability of supers to motivate some of their people is likely to lead to high-performance contracting units. Also, sheer aggressiveness by corps of highly talented managers and specialists will make the supers successful in getting a high proportion of the contracts they try for.

The qualitative advantages of the contract state would be supported by supers more than by most conventional corporations or the conglomerates we have known. New ventures are a large part of what supercorporations are all about, and these ventures must include qualitative differences; thus, the supers are tooled for making quality contributions to the operation of the contract state. This visible and credible capability will both add momentum to the contracting movement and increase its efficacy. That is a considerable contribution, even for supercorporations.

Moreover, supercorporations, as we saw in Part Two, would tend to be more competitive, in more lines of business. Being better geared to compete, the supers would respond well to the government-industry competition that is one of the safeguards of the contracting system. Supers' competition would be mainly in innovation and in cost effectiveness. With these pursued as a way of life, the supercorporations would be among the greatest competitors in whatever new, suitable, and profitable contracts governments may award. As such, the supers would participate prominently in the qualitative competition, helping to find smarter ways to do some of the public business.

A more conventional business once again supplies an advance look at what supercorporations can contribute to the quality of performance of government services by profit-making corporations. A real estate investment trust is integrating the races in housing, with no riots, no lawsuits, no subsidies, no bureaucrats, just good housing and good profits. The organization, Mutual Real Estate Investment Trust, has a total of $25 million worth of apartments in 15 properties in eight states. Mutual Real Estate buys all-white units and gradually integrates them. This is a small real estate investment trust, to be sure, but it works on a regular basis, without the support of the contract state. It has made, within its means, an innovative, qualitative difference—and this before the contract state and supercorporations arrive on the scene with immensely larger resources.

Regarding the disadvantages of the corporate state not already touched upon with respect to supers, there is no predicting how either the supercorporations or the contract state will fare with organized labor. The estimated strength of supers in dealing with their employees through both traditional and innovative concepts and techniques may also work with unions, or it may not. We must thus leave moot the labor point relative to the supers' contributions to the contract state.

It is possible that the disadvantages of supercorporations will, oddly, enable them to overcome some of the other disadvantages of the contract state: excessive politicking; crass inappropriateness in the treatment of people served; nefarious bargaining for contracts; and totalitarian tendencies. In what way do the supers' disadvantages help? The relevant disadvantages are extreme visibility, the emotional bias that equates bigness with badness, the negative reaction to wide diversification that puts a large corporate finger into many pies, the unusual efficiency that alerts skeptics and critics, and the rapid growth that excites private envy and public scrutiny.

If the supers never did anything wrong—an unlikely event—they would still be among the most probed organizations in this or any other society. This is a searing disadvantage for them. The other side of the coin is that the supers will thereby be rendered less capable of (and perhaps less interested in) committing overt sins. This "Caesar's wife" effect specifically applies to the four disadvantages of the contract state mentioned above.

Supercorporations will be wrong and do wrong on all too many occasions. However, it beggars belief that their managers will be front-runners in the kinds of major league gamesmanship that would damage badly the processes of the contract state. Any management that will have to fight Washington for up to several years just to get approval for a small acquisition that would be unquestioned for a smaller acquirer is not, it seems, a hot candidate for excessive politicking, too-clever bargaining, and all the rest.

Finally, the loss of large-scale voluntary services is a threat of serious dimensions. In some cases, a supercorporation will have to forgo otherwise good contracting propositions, possibly in favor of smaller and less inflammatory competitors. In other cases—and this leads to another super strength—it may find a way of structuring a group of profit and nonprofit entities that satisfies the several natural interests in the service and its contracting. We have said that supercorporations will be far more adept than many others in structuring new modes of ventures. Their expected multiple captives and their joint ventures, among others, will provide experience and appetite for new forms and combinations of profit and nonprofit groupings.

I predict that by the 1980s the contracting of government services to businesses may increase greatly in variety, and in volume by at least several billions of dollars per year. This movement into the contract state may go further, and by 1990 could produce stupendous increases in business contracting and decreases in the size of government bureaucracies.

Whatever the extent of the contract state, it will provide a complex of advantages and disadvantages too new to be fully sorted out this early in the game. We can see that some of the advantages of the contract state will be comprehensive increases in the effectiveness, efficiency, and quality of the contracted services, plus a distinct increase in the strength of business competition and business-government competition. The predictable disadvantages of the contract state are certain inherent inefficiencies, possibly inhumane services to people, too much politics, possible labor objections, the possible loss of mammoth amounts of existing volunteer work, and a potentially totalitarian bent.

The advantages should outweigh the disadvantages of the contract state. If so, the supercorporations' characteristic efficiency, competitiveness, and sensitive managements will help to make it work passably well. Moreover, for better or worse, the presence of supercorporations will accelerate the movement of our postindustrial society into the contract state.

15

THE THIRD WORLD and the SUPER WORLD

THE NIGHTMARES of our own society have their more primitive versions in the emerging countries. One of the more threatening of all the world's social concerns is the failure of the less developed countries to develop. The misery and frustration of these countries and the concern and perplexity of the more developed nations are quietly eating away at the peace of all. In the more developed nations, the energy crisis, the confusion and alienation of their citizens, and the gloom of daily headlines are hiding the worsening plight of the less developed countries.

At the same time, the size and nature of the less developed countries make them very large areas of potential opportunity in the distant future, both for themselves and for most other countries. The ultimate potential values to mankind of these countries and their people should prove to be even more enormous than their immediate problems.

But the less developed nations are not making it today. Robert S. McNamara, president of the International Bank for Reconstruction and Development (the World Bank), said in October 1972 that all the aid given to less developed countries during the postwar era had failed to have any significant impact on the "hundreds of millions" of people of these lands. This confirms, on a world scale, Gunnar Myrdal's specific finding of five years earlier that the societies of the less developed nations of Asia were disintegrating under the load of their population explosions. If billions of dollars in aid to less developed countries have not helped the people, and if there are increasing differences in aspirations and interests between the developed nations and the Third World, why should supercorporations try to do anything at all?

"Benign neglect," as Dr. Daniel P. Moynihan once phrased it in another matter, is a tempting attitude for the so-called developed nations. After all, the futurist Herman Kahn has assured us that in 100 years the world's affluence will have funded the solutions to all economic problems, including those of the less developed countries. Their populations, along with all others, are predicted to have an average annual income per capita of $10,000.

Two things are wrong with benign neglect. First, the less developed countries have alarming problems that must be solved before the predicted bonanza 100 years from now. Second, as events in the United States during the 1960s must have shown, economic affluence does not guarantee either domestic or international tranquility.

Consequently, some conclude that more productive actions to support the efforts of the less developed countries are essential to the underlying welfare of all nations. It is to those thus persuaded that this discussion will be of greatest interest. Additionally, the discussion should be of interest to those investors and managers who wish to consider further the hazards and profit potentials of less developed countries as they relate to supercorporations.

Let us shunt aside a series of basic issues that least concern us in the relationship between supercorporations and the less developed countries: the primarily governmental and political aids to these nations; the question of whether they are responsibly helping themselves—considering, for example, their nearly total failure to control extreme population increases; the objective soundness of certain of their policies, including expropriation; their downgrading of environmental priorities; some extreme nationalism; the failure of economy-wide gains to filter down to the masses; and certain other issues that do not lend themselves to private sector treatment.

Without this much of the meat of the matter, there remain the hotly festering problems of how supercorporations and other companies can live with the less developed nations as they are and may be in the future. The difficulty, as we have hinted, is partly one of different aspirations and interests.

Conflicting Aspirations and Interests

Whether wise or otherwise, the less developed countries make it clear that they do not want to be just like us. They do not intend to maximize economic efficiency in every case that conflicts with their own social priorities. One of the many deeply felt statements of differences in aspirations was made by a Nigerian professor, J. Ade Oyelabi. He is convinced that the normal corporate drive for the worldwide economic efficiency of each profit center—a prime value of multinational operations—subverts the equally natural needs of less developed countries. Typical corporate decisions may interfere with the host country's higher priorities for full employment and what is locally regarded as fair distribution of income.

Also, other opinion leaders in these nations object to the export of their natural resources. Further, the greater expertise of Americans and other nationals is widely believed to be an enduring obstacle to the development of business skills by the citizens of the less developed countries.

A fifth categorical difference in aspirations is concerned with specific investments or projects. Those of highest profit potential in the corporate sense may be of much less interest to the host country, and may divert the host country's resources from projects of national value to those which are seen to benefit mostly affluent absentee owners.

A sixth difference in aspirations that separates these countries from the more developed nations and corporations is the balancing of environmental concerns with the need for economic growth. At the 1972 UN conference on environment in Stockholm, and elsewhere, it became more evident that less developed countries sometimes want economic growth emphasized, even at the price of preventable pollution of their environments. This feeling is surfacing at the same time that the more developed countries are building environmental protection from a rump movement into a major claimant in their capital investment programs.

Japan ignored a series of air and water pollution problems while it changed, in five years, from the World Bank's largest borrower to its largest lender. Now Japan is planning to commit the equivalent of a trillion dollars to a transformation of its society and economy by 1985. A multi-billion-dollar portion of this revolutionary movement will be dedicated to cleaning up the previously neglected problems of pollution. The United States had already begun similar multi-billion-dollar investments, and other more developed nations are following suit.

Influencing these six radically different and internally inconsistent aspirations is the tendency of some intellectuals and others in less developed nations toward a Marxist view of society and economics. Mr. Oyelabi, the Nigerian academic quoted earlier, has an apparently Marxist attitude of the "exploitation" of these countries by the powerful corporations of the more developed nations.

The conflict in aspirations and interests is not corroborated by a UN study of the operations of multinational U.S. enterprises in less developed countries. This study, by Dr. Raymond Vernon of the Harvard Business School, sympathizes with the noneconomic feelings of vulnerability and lack of control over their own destinies that are obviously felt by leaders of these nations. However, in economic terms, Dr. Vernon finds that these countries have, subject to further study, generally profited from the activities of multinational U.S. corporations within their borders.

Notwithstanding these reassuring economic indications, the seven foregoing differences in aspirations and interests are an awesome barrier to any efforts, profit-making or charitable, by supercorporations. This wall is buttressed by the fashionable rage against multinational corporations, by which is often meant U.S. multinational corporations. Given the indeterminate life-span of such international opinion, it is possible that multinational companies may be under active attack for perhaps the remainder of the 1970s.

SUPERCORPORATE INTERESTS

The emerging supercorporations will not run into the crusade against multinational corporations until perhaps 1978. It is clear now that the supers are to be visibly more effective versions of the already villainous multinationals. Therefore, one possibility is that supercorporations may inadvertently add their own high-octane fuel to an already hot fire.

This possibility leads to several conclusions that are both significant and negative. First, perhaps the multinational tentacles of supers should be drawn in, or cropped, to minimize the expected collision with those groups already in hot pursuit of the often less aggressive, nonsuper multinationals. Second, perhaps the supers should also avoid opening up contacts and initiatives with the less developed countries, by policy confining their elegant plans to the more developed nations.

Third, and more specifically, the supers perhaps should shun opportunities to contribute, on a subnormal profit basis, to solutions to the problems of the less developed countries. Such contributions, regardless of any altruistic intent, could unnecessarily push supercorporations into the cross fire that has already broken out between these nations and the more conventional multinationals. The future of supercorporations might thus be secured in part by their attempts to stay free and clear of this hostility that is a brew of racial, economic, social, religious, and national differences in aspirations. If these negative conclusions prevail, then the supers would have only nominal or occasional new relationships with the more than 100 less developed countries.

To this barrier to supercorporate efforts, which originates with less developed countries, must be added the predictably negative reactions of executives of supercorporations. They would be less than human if they were not inclined to stay out of noisome and dangerous situations. Viewing only the foregoing negative aspects, they would probably see neither economic nor humane grounds for intentionally walking over the hot coals of these nations' antipathy. They would no doubt find other, less hostile camps into which they could more constructively move their profit-making and social efforts—including underdeveloped areas of the otherwise more developed nations. After all, Japan is not only one of the world's leading economic powers, it is also a place where only about 15 percent of the population of 100 million has any sewage facilities. The United States, we know, has millions of people with unrealized potential. There are obviously greener pastures for the supers than the less developed countries, with their present attitudes toward more developed nations and corporations.

This skimming of the antithetical views and aspirations of less developed nations and large corporations, including supers, could be a preview of the actual world of the later 1970s and the 1980s. Both emotion and profit logic can point us in this direction. Nevertheless, the futurist, knowing that he does not know the future, must at least search all sides of the issues. Sometimes he may come down on the side of comity and progress—as unfashionable as such conclusions may be.

We can detect some basis for less than total segregation of super-corporations from the less developed countries. At the broadest philosophical level, we may remember Dr. Dennis Gabor's memorable phrase, "We cannot predict the future, but we can invent the future." Although Sir Dennis did not use this optimistic thought in connection with the less developed nations, it may be fitting in relation to them. Ways may be found of helping to solve their problems that would accommodate their felt national necessities as well as the strategic planning and profit criteria of supercorporations. Thus, supers might not be consigned to a ramlike butting of heads with the less developed countries, nor to extreme isolation from them. We may discover a series of creative new starting points.

For example, the governmental development corporation of one small and poor African nation has shaped its own approach to filling the shortage of businessmen with advanced corporate experience and skills. The approach was still exploratory at the time that the managing director of the development corporation wrote to me about the concept in these terms:

> [Our country is] almost completely lacking in the kinds of institutions that its development requires and we see one of our key jobs as creating them. . . . We are attempting to spawn subsidiaries (as joint ventures, if possible) in key economic areas. We are interested in establishing . . . a property management and development firm, a national transportation company, a tourist development corporation, and an agro-industrial development corporation. . . .
>
> Clearly, we can't do all of this ourselves. . . . To solve all of the above, I would like to create a subsidiary . . . which would have the majority of its shares owned by us and a minority owned by some firm with the standing and with the experience we need to achieve all of the above objectives. *We* [emphasis added] would be responsible for funding the various projects, obtaining feasibility surveys from donor agencies, and acting as blocking back with the various government agencies. . . . Our partner would be responsible for keeping the business properly staffed, and for providing the expert backing that the staff may need from time to time.
>
> The partner would benefit in two ways: one is that bright young men in the partner's organization could get firing-line experience earlier than usual and therefore their worth will be increased; the second is that the partner can deal himself in on a few projects on a locally equitable basis—returns are fairly exciting in property here.

Pretty good for a new African country. Pretty good, too, as a working example of the kind of innovative effort that is needed to get around the strongly opposed aspirations of less developed countries and supers and other profit-making corporations.

The reality of these bridge-building ideas and the promise of still unborn ideas allow for a future of cooperation between less developed nations and supercorporations. In fact, the heralded creativity and aggressiveness of the supers, plus the global need for greater accomplishment in the Third World, are the basis for predicting that the obstacles to super contributions will be increasingly overcome in perhaps half of the 100 less developed countries, and that those supercorporations which are also multinational will make more than their share of contributions and profits.

This optimistic prediction is not justified by today's facts, nor by a straight-line projection of them. Instead, it is based on the faith that a change will be ground out by the flexibility of some multinational corporations, sparked by the supers, and encouraged by more pragmatic leadership in many less developed nations. There may well be a reciprocal change in the attitudes, if not in the oratory, of the leaders of some 50 of them. All these advances will be over and above the certain reverse actions of Third World cartels, nationalizations, sporadic harassments, embargos, and other problems that may arise as these countries mature.

Rich Versus Poor

One of the now obvious economic differences between a few of the less developed countries and the more developed nations will also have a big impact on all parties. A handful of Arab countries has amassed tens of billions of dollars' worth of capital from oil payments from the United States, Europe, Japan, and the Third World. Their hoard of foreign currency reserves is expected to total hundreds of billions in the next ten years. The foreseeable effects of these reserves on large corporations, and vice versa, have only just begun to be considered other than in their currency-market operations and other current commitments. These effects can be simply divided into those within the oil-rich Middle Eastern countries and those within the United States and other countries that will house supercorporations.

Most of the oil-rich Arab lands are much less developed than many other countries, such as a number of those in Latin America. Illiteracy is widespread. It is not reasonable to think that nearly all the oil dollars will be clamped into vaults, to be used for investing in companies listed on the New York, Frankfurt, and other leading stock exchanges. Some still undetermined portion of the fabulous oil income can be used for improving the lot of the people of these oil-rich but otherwise dirt-poor countries. Schools and hospitals and roads and housing are obvious and capital-intensive uses to which the surpluses can be put. All kinds of corporations—contractors, material suppliers, equipment manufacturers, and many others—can count on receiving some of this business.

The more speculative but challenging possibility is that supercorporations and other companies may create and deliver new kinds of products and services that will multiply the growth of these rich/poor countries on a scale of effectiveness not yet seen in the postwar foreign aid and trade operations. Some such corporate ventures have been tried, such as the unsuccessful development attempt promoted by Litton Industries in Greece. More needs to be learned, and the macrosystems needed for further development could be devised only by quite large, advanced, financially sophisticated corporations, something like supercorporations.

Perhaps the waves made in the United States and elsewhere by Arab oil wealth will be mitigated by the amount of new, sensible opportunities for investment in the Arab nations created by large and responsible corporations. More school desks, trucks, and x-ray equipment, by themselves, will clearly not diminish the hoard of oil profits to livable proportions. Rather, a few multi-billion-dollar programs to raise the oil countries' capabilities to advance their people and to develop other industries—thus reducing their almost total dependence on oil—can be one of the most sensible movements for all concerned. Several developed countries, including France and Japan, have already signed multi-billion-dollar industrial development contracts with Arab oil countries. This opens the field for some supercorporations to follow with major development deals of their own.

On the other side of the coin, many tens of billions of dollars' worth of funds will still be loose and looking for a home. Unsettling thoughts of direct Arab take-overs of a string of American and other corporations have been voiced. The market value of most publicly held companies, and nearly all privately held companies, happens to be less than one billion dollars each. *Forbes* has calculated, in a bear market, that the entire U.S. metals industry, including steel, aluminum, copper, and lead, has a market value of only $20 billion. The transportation industry is listed and quoted at $17 billion. Industrial equipment manufacturing—all of it—is priced on today's securities markets at a paltry $10 billion. Even to imagine the Bethlehem Steels, the American Airlines, and the Babcock & Wilcoxes owned and controlled by very different foreign interests, eight to eleven time zones away, stirs up quite a reaction, doesn't it? When we remember that some of the Middle Eastern countries are coup prone, our reactions become aggravated.

One can hope that the money managers of the Middle East will behave "responsibly" in *our* terms. The record thus far is mixed. It has been reported in *The Wall Street Journal* and elsewhere that Arab money has placed a staggering load on the drooping U.S. dollar. Kuwait, Saudi Arabia, and Libya, among others, threw hundreds of millions of dollars onto the currency markets and contributed directly to at least one of the devaluations of the dollar. This is not to criticize the ethics of the Arab countries in their currency dealings. Instead, it is a factual observation of the differing needs and interests of these countries relative to the United States and other more developed nations. A partial defusing of the unusual wealth of these few less developed countries may result from the normal operations of the forthcoming supercorporations, as well as from the frontier opportunities in the Middle East itself.

SUPERCORPORATIONS AND THE OIL-RICH COUNTRIES

Supercorporations—at least some of them—will be generically poor in capital. They are likely to develop more profitable new ventures than can be readily financed in a capital-short world. One solution to this supercorporate problem already being used increasingly is to tap the surplus capital sources outside Europe. Starting with Japan, this trend has accelerated into the Arab countries. Japanese capital has been used to fund such big U.S. corporations as Chrysler and General Telephone and Electronics. In a more complex deal, a bank based in Nassau, the Bahamas, that is a subsidiary of the large Italian energy corporation ENI, was financed for 50 million West German marks (equivalent to more than U.S. $14 million) through nine financial organizations, six of which were Japanese.

The financial and business ties between the developed nations and the Arab countries that I have predicted for supercorporations and others had early help from the likes of the J. P. Morgan Overseas Capital Corp. In 1973 it acquired 40 percent of the stock of Bank Al-mashrek S.A.L. of Beirut, Lebanon. Among the directors of Bank Al-mashrek are nominees of the states of Kuwait and Qatar and the Republic of Lebanon.

The expanding practice of the Arabs and others of financing of some of the capital needs of U.S. corporations may be a boon. The corporations get necessary capital that would otherwise be less available and more costly. The Arabs gain employment for their dollars and other currencies that should be more profitable and stable than speculating or trading in currencies—a trade in which there are many losers. The world's trading nations would benefit as a group from any moderation of the severe currency tempests of the early 1970s. The really poor less developed countries would be less buffeted by major currency devaluations, revaluations, joint floats, and what have you. Total calm will never reign, but any less frenetic existence would remove some of the burrs from under the saddles of both government and business managers and allow them to think more about less developed nations and other social concerns.

The place of supercorporations in all this can be easily imagined. First, their size and rapid growth will make them strong absorbers of some of the excess reserves of Arab and other capital-rich countries. Second, the supers ought to figure among the more attractive investment opportunities for foreign-owned (as well as domestic) capital, principally because of their projected high rates of profitability and growth, but also because of strengths of scale. This inherent attractiveness means that the supers are likely to get more than their share from the otherwise wandering caravans of Arab currency hoards.

The third point is more problematic and also more interesting. Because of the flexibility of the supers to engage in all sorts of ventures and partnerships, they may attract still more of the Arab currency reserves now being used for speculation. In addition to the more conventional investment arrangements implied in point two, there could also be some more aggressive joint ventures or special partnerships between supers and Arab money managers.

One off-the-cuff example is some kind of joint equity participation in new housing in Europe, funded partly by Arabs and partly by one or more supercorporations, with the venture conceived and implemented mainly by the supers. Another is a consortium for mining Australian bauxite or for tree farming in Latin America. The investment-poor Arabs would not always be straight lenders or merely purchasers of some listed stock. Instead, they would be venture partners, risking some very large sums in business undertakings that would be less feasible without their supplying part of the equity capital. Although this is the most speculative of the alternatives I see for excess Arab wealth, this alternative could prove to be of immense value to many of the less developed countries.

Intermediate Technology

We must not forget that over 90 percent of the population of the less developed nations lives in groaningly poor countries with few reserves and with capital needs on a scale never before seen in their parts of the world. We are consequently further concerned to see how supercorporations can relate to these countries. Let us analyze one of the specific means by which they can work together on a day-to-day and people-to-people basis.

For one of the most discussed ideas on this subject, we are indebted to the articulate Dutch economist Andre van Dam, director of planning for Latin America for CPC International, Inc., who has collected and presented a body of information on "intermediate technology." This phrase refers to all forms of technology that are more advanced than primitive tools but less advanced than the contemporary state of the art in the technologically advanced nations. Dr. van Dam uses a two-wheeled, walk-behind tractor as an illustration. This is a simple implement that could have been made in the advanced nations some 70 years ago, and that is useful in today's less developed countries. It is intermediate between the water buffalo and today's best agricultural tractors, complete with air conditioning and power steering.

Both conventional corporations and other groups, such as the Intermediate Technology Group in London, have been fostering the idea and the hardware of intermediate technology. A quick review of the concept and some examples are needed before we can comment on the role supercorporations may play in this field. The concept is another result of the opposition between the aspirations of the less developed nations and the conventional wisdom of the more advanced countries and corporations. The lively interest in the Third World in using intermediate, rather than advanced, technology seems to spring as much from a social and political desire to employ the unemployed as from economics. As we noted earlier, unemployment is a principal concern of many leaders of these countries.

Also, we have recognized that most of these nations—over 90 of them—are exceedingly short of capital for development. The walk-behind tractor can be fabricated locally with the most elementary materials and tools, thus providing still more employment, while supplying a form of tractor that costs a fraction of the price of the regular commercial product. These countries can, if they wish, have tens of thousands more of the walk-behind units than they could of the most sophisticated machines demanded in the advanced countries.

Dr. van Dam has already found an impressive number of other products and processes that stem from the concept of intermediate technology. One Japanese glass company operating in India manages to use six times as many workers as it does in a comparable plant in its highly developed homeland. A Dutch multinational corporation uses a pilot plant as a means of learning how to scale down its advanced technologies to levels that suit the less developed countries. It has simplified a multipurpose offset printing press from its advanced original and sells the press for one-fourth the original price.

Deliberately minimizing economic efficiency in countries that are desperately in need of building sufficient capital for their survival may be a questionable policy, and there may be other endemic problems with intermediate technology. But so long as the less developed nations embrace it in theory and in practice, intermediate technology will be with us. With this in mind, what does an extremely advanced company contribute, if anything?

THE SUPERCORPORATE PUSH

Supercorporations may bring a new dimension to intermediate technology. The less developed nations need not only such special hardware but also more and better delivery and applications systems. For example, systems that will get the glass factory and the cut-down offset press into their countries and into use. The rare traits of scale and ingenuity, to be combined in the supercorporations, can be expected to provide some of the push that will get more of the delivery and applications jobs done.

Take a hypothetical example, one that may not remain hypothetical. We have known for too long that about one-fourth of all the food raised by the less developed countries is never consumed—not by their malnourished people, that is. One potential meal in every four is consumed or otherwise destroyed by birds, bugs, and blight, or rots for lack of adequate transportation or storage.

There are some twentieth-century remedies and also some simpler ones. A twentieth-century remedy was the almost total destruction of the desert locust, *Schistocerca gregaria,* the same locust that in biblical times "covered the face of the whole land, so that the land was darkened. . . ." The UN's desert-locust project put squadrons of aircraft to work spraying insecticides selectively over areas aggregating more than 11 million square miles. By 1969, the desert locust was almost entirely eradicated. That was nine years after the airborne combat began, but several thousand years after people began fighting the invading locusts with brooms, firebrands, and the beating of drums.

Supercorporations can add much intermediate technology to the saving of one meal in every four, in addition to the advanced attacks that are also needed. Taking in some cases a systems approach, a super can first pinpoint the causes for losing a quarter of the native foodstuffs, allowing for the many national and regional variations. Next, it can determine what remedies will most reduce the losses. Remedies, still hypothetical at this point, may include low-cost storage sheds, elementary mechanical loading devices, or a simplified bag manufacturing plant.

Whatever the answers, the next step may represent the special contribution of the supercorporation: help in marshalling available public and private resources in the less developed country, plus other aid, plus some of the super's own resources. A determined drive over, say, a ten-year period could perhaps do as much to reduce tragic food losses with intermediate technology as advanced technology did by liquidating the desert locust.

Supercorporations not being charitable institutions, what is in it for the supers themselves? Depending on the basic businesses of the super, it may earn its required rates of profit in two or more of the following four ways (related to the example we have been using). (1) The super's systems group may increase its business by putting together an overall pattern for reducing the huge losses of foods. (2) A joint venture between a super and a less developed country may increase its business volume by manufacturing and erecting hundreds of thousands or even millions of storage sheds. (This isn't like manufacturing lasers, or MIRVs for nuclear warheads, but the profits can be there.) (3) A lot of profit may be involved in the joint-venture production of the simple mechanical loaders, construction of the bag manufacturing plants, or manufacture of whatever capital goods are required for the programmed solution. (4) Zeroing in on the often missing delivery and applications systems, a super might make money by directing the programs needed to teach the native employees how to manage and operate the new food-saving systems and hardware.

This hypothetical commitment of supercorporations to pushing intermediate technology solutions to the age-old problem of monstrous and preventable food losses in countries with starving populations may sound too idealistic. Before you reach this conclusion, however, recall that the Rockefeller-sponsored International Basic Economy Corporation (IBEC) has already achieved, profitably, some marvelous results in less developed countries.

For example, IBEC's Poultry Group has grossed as much as $62 million a year and netted some $2 million profit by introducing improved breeding stock to 23 countries on five continents. IBEC also handles end-product marketing of chickens and eggs in some of these relatively primitive economies. This additional boost, in turn, has encouraged more of the people in remote rural areas to start raising poultry for the first time. The mighty Rockefellers, through IBEC, are thus doing such humble things as training illiterate poultry farmers and helping them get a little start-up money.

This and other humble ventures have been established in less developed countries on a profitable basis by a company that does not yet begin to approach supercorporate size, strength, or diversity. (IBEC's 1973 sales were $312 million, profits $2.3 million.) This comparison of sizes takes nothing from IBEC, which is one of the jewels of the free enterprise system. It does, however, give weight to the argument that the emerging supercorporations can make new inroads into raising the technological effectiveness of less developed countries through powerful applications of the sounder aspects of intermediate technology.

Now, to summarize my predictions of the interactions between supercorporations and the more than 100 less developed countries. Most of these countries are not making it. They may even be falling below their own precariously low development standards, as their rapid population growth threatens the meager progress they have made. The world's experts and supporters of development in these countries are discouraged, if not stumped.

It is presumptuous to predict that a small number of U.S. and other supercorporations will necessarily make any greater gains than have the combined efforts of governments, the UN, the private sector, and nongovernmental organizations. However, it is probable that the supercorporations can and will share in increasing undertakings to break the poverty cycle of perhaps half of the less developed nations. More than likely, there will be a fluid but tolerable degree of peace between many of these countries and the supers, primed by flashes of creativity on both sides of the development fence. This conditional peace, based on ideas and aspirations, will allow a pace and degree of development that might help reverse the postwar trend in about half of the less developed countries of the world.

The dealings between supercorporations and the rich/poor countries may fall into two realizable and worthwhile categories. First, supers can help nations with very poor populations and very large reserves of currency and gold to develop their people and their economies, in part with ordinary products and services, but more with new macrosystems for advancing people and diversifying these dangerously one-product economies.

Second, supercorporations will attract some portion of the reserves now feverishly being used for speculation into mutually profitable investments. Some of the investments thus induced will help to make long-range equity partners in great ventures out of the hot money players of today. Some of these ventures are likely to be of direct value to other, poorer, less developed countries. These two results will be byproducts of the normal business activities of supercorporations.

It is quite likely that the supers will add substance and creativity to the desired spread of intermediate technology in these nations. Public and private participants have already produced ingenious hardware that more nearly fits the very limited capital of these nations, while employing more of their otherwise unemployed citizens in the building of farms, businesses, and whole economies. The supercorporations may add the muscle of large scale and the determination of the entrepreneur on a regional or worldwide front. The extremely humble tasks are not to be laughed off. They have already been shown to provide results acceptable to the least developed areas and peoples, while also racking up multi-million-dollar profits.

It is equally likely that supercorporations will add to the advanced technology programs that are also essential to the development of these countries. In all this, the supers will be adding to their own growth and profitability and helping to make productive the now unstable piles of excess currency reserves in oil-rich Arab nations. We cannot expect supercorporations by themselves to resolve the dilemma of the less developed countries, but it is important to both the supers and these countries that they begin by perceiving a core of mutual advantage. This needed beginning can attenuate natural hostility and lead to useful gains for supers and some of the first real gains for the people of the less developed countries.

16

SUPERCORPORATIONS and NEW CITIES

THE CREATION OF NEW CITIES is the fourth sociocorporate movement by which supercorporations may throw great weight into the fight against many of our familiar social problems.

Some socially oriented activities would satisfy some of those who side with Dr. Milton Friedman. These are the programs that are both money-making and tied to solutions of social problems. One gargantuan example is the building of new cities largely or wholly by the private sector. For example, Urban Investment Development Co., a subsidiary of Aetna Life & Casualty Co., is heading a group of nongovernmental developers in creating a new city west of Chicago. The new city, to be called Fox Valley East, will cost a billion dollars. It is to have a population of 50,000 to be housed in some 20,000 homes and apartment units.

There are at least a dozen new cities of the largest size, as Fox Valley East is planned to be. But the fact is that new cities, which we are trumpeting as a leading new vehicle for solving some social concerns, are in trouble before they have been fairly tried out. It has been reported that nearly all are not doing well financially. Columbia, Maryland, is a bright exception. Columbia, among other accomplishments, has attracted industry on its own exacting terms. General Electric has chosen Columbia for the site of a large new appliance manufacturing center, for example. Columbia appears to be getting every ounce of value from its situation. It even produces additional income from a series of seminars and programs for those wanting to learn about profitably planning, building, and operating new cities.

Aside from Columbia and one or two others, new cities are in serious trouble. Because hundreds of millions to billions of dollars must be committed for each new city, the potential losses from faltering new cities are big enough to scare off the largest and boldest supercorporations and other large corporations. On the basis of their track record to date, we might conclude that this new vehicle is stalled, perhaps permanently. But there is more to the story.

Even without the advent of supercorporations there would nevertheless be a strong case for the future of new cities. This case rests on several fundamental factors. First, there is an extreme need for, and interest in, new cities. According to a 1969 conference of leading planners, 110 entirely new cities will be needed in the future. Additional large corporations are continuing to go into the business, some on an entirely private-enterprise basis. Next, an analysis of the reasons for the losses and failures in the first generation of new cities indicates that some of them are remediable within the framework of sound cities and sound business. Moreover, the corporations founding new cities are likely to receive strong government support, especially in financing and land acquisition. Some combination of these factors can be expected to advance the concept of new cities as a wholesale means of resolving some of our social concerns in the postindustrial society.

The Potentials of New Cities

To visualize the interrelationship between supercorporations and new cities, assume that large new cities will continue to be planned and built in the 1970s and 1980s. A sampling of the nature and special features of two of them will lay a base for further sensing the natural affinity of supers and new cities. The two new cities are Fox Valley East and Minnesota Experimental City (MXC).

Fox Valley East is the more usual of the two in that it is a satellite city for the Chicago area rather than a stand-alone new city, as is MXC. The last of the 50,000 people of Fox Valley East are expected to have moved in by 1995. Financing of almost the entire venture is to be by private enterprise. The only exceptions, which its principal sponsor, Urban Investment and Development Co., noted to me, are the possibility of governmental aid to help provide housing for lower income families, and the possibility of governmental open-space grants. These exceptions leave Fox Valley East a billion-dollar private enterprise. Urban Investment and Development assures me that Fox Valley East is programmed to produce normal rates of profitability, and thus it is not to be a sacrificial offering by its sponsors.

One of my great interests is the prospering of small businesses in an economy of giants. In Fox Valley East it is possible that smaller businesses may become important participants in such aspects as the development of portions of residential areas and the industrial development of the new city.

The five-way partnership for Fox Valley East has underlying assets amounting to tens of billions of dollars. The managing partner, Urban Investment and Development, is, as noted, a wholly owned subsidiary of Aetna Life & Casualty Co. The other four partners, each a power in its own right, are Homart Development Co., a subsidiary of Sears, Roebuck; Mafco, Inc., a subsidiary of Marshall Field; Metropolitan Structures; and Henry Crown and Co.

These five have the following goals and plans in response to social concerns:

— Fox Valley East is anticipated to be both racially and economically integrated.
— A range of housing types will be provided for most income levels. Some of the jobs being created in the community will be filled by people of minimal skills. The developers are making it possible for these people, as well as others, to live in the new city, near their work.
— The new city will have socially beneficial health programs for all residents.
— A small stream is to be converted into a series of interlocking lakes that will also serve as a flood-control facility. These lakes and other planned open spaces are to be linked with existing and proposed forest preserves and hiking trails, thus creating a regional open-space and park facility.
— The developers are not only providing a sewage disposal system and a water system, they are also assuring that there will be adequate funding for these environmentally valuable facilities.

— The variety and efficacy of land uses are planned to provide a stable tax base that should add to the strength of the tax base of the entire related area.
— The entire new city is to proceed from a high quality of planning, with the potential of raising, by example, the standards and the future performance of other urban planning in nearby areas.

Of the concerned citizens, of the experts reading this book, does anyone know of any other vehicle that even purports to deal so effectively with seven major social concerns? All these high goals and concrete plans for specific performance are glued together with private enterprise, at normal profit standards, too.

Now, a briefer look at Minnesota Experimental City. The plans for an advanced new city in northern Minnesota will suggest the grand dimensions and problems of the new-city movement and its special interaction with the arriving supercorporations. MXC is to be located on 50,000 acres in Aitkin County, over 100 miles north of Minneapolis-St. Paul. Construction is to start in 1975, with completion about 1985. The maximum population of MXC is set at 250,000, making it one of the largest of the U.S. new cities to date. The cost: $8 billion to $12 billion.

MXC is one of the relatively few new cities planned as an independent urban center; most others are satellites or new suburbs. Other head-turning concepts for MXC include a totally enclosed, climate-conditioned downtown district; remote shopping at home by cable TV; and driverless minibuses. Some businessmen are already seeing MXC as a test center for new products and services, as well as a profitable market for their current offerings. MXC is not as far along as Fox Valley East, but it is reaching for still further new, vital ideas and methods.

The Pitfalls of New Cities

These two new cities were deliberately selected as examples to convey the shining promise of new cities as a vehicle for dealing meaningfully with a range of social concerns, as well as for making money in a traditional, free-market manner. Against these examples stand the deep hazards that have rarely been overcome and that will require the best of supercorporations and other large corporations to avoid in the future.

For one thing, ensuring the social success of new cities is difficult. Reports on Reston, Virginia, one of the pioneers in the field, make it all too plain that many of the same old social problems move into the new cities along with the residents. Certainly the new cities start out with no slum property and no ghetto concentrations of minority people. The land use can be well planned, and pollution of air, water, and noise can be generally prevented. Schools can provide adequate and equal access to learning opportunities. Nevertheless, something goes wrong, for broken homes and drug abuse and juvenile delinquency and other contemporary ills exist in Reston, and in most, if not all, other new cities. New cities will be designed and built anyway. But the persistence, at least in this generation, of societal ills will be a severe problem for the sponsors, as well as for the citizens, of the emergent cities.

A second and worsening problem is that of future financing, generally, and of land acquisition, in particular. The prices of raw and developed land continue to rise, along with increasing construction costs. Also, some economists expect a sustained secular rise in the cost of capital. And the accumulating social demands for living space for low income and unemployable people may put a further strain on both financing and land acquisition for the new cities.

A third pitfall may be corporate meddling in local politics. Huge corporations, including supers, will have many negative aspects, both real and imagined. Corporate sponsors may well be involved in political meddling with, or domination of, their new cities. This would be a natural reaction: any self-respecting corporate manager would be expected to do whatever can reasonably be done to protect or enhance his investment and the returns on it. It may be that a handy lever for moving the new city in the right corporate direction will lie in its local political machinery.

A turn of events such as this could tarnish the householder's interest in moving to, or remaining in, an otherwise livable new city. This potential threat to the still stumbling new-city movement is one of the numerous reasons for caution about supercorporations. Neither optimism nor pessimism should be automatic. With early warnings such as this one, a few alert citizens of the new cities may be able to head off corporate political machines before they get rolling.

Supercorporate Sponsorship

This short catalog of the potentials and pitfalls of new cities holds the door partly open for the largest and most competent entrepreneurs and managers. The already apparent problems of even large, competent sponsors of new cities invite a comparison with the expected new-city ventures of the supercorporations. Assuming conservatively that one or more such super ventures will fail, we may wonder what could make most of them into winners?

At least four of the requirements for supercorporations will make a difference. First, into this capital-intensive business of new cities the supers will bring an above-average efficiency in the obtaining and management of capital. Part One sketched the considerable differences between capital costs based on older, conventional financial and operating policies and capital costs based on a more efficient use of capital. Less conventional policies were shown to result in lower costs for equity capital and an ability to obtain capital with less dilution of equity.

A second characteristic that will bolster the supercorporations' chances of succeeding in new-city ventures is, perhaps unexpectedly, their penchant for getting into and out of ventures. Not every place is the right place for a new city, and not every concept will attract the needed minimum residential and business population. The supers will be able to maneuver themselves more adroitly out of doomed new-city ventures. They will also be able to move more quickly into potentially good ventures for new cities. Commitments to large tracts of land, lining up partners, setting up the development concepts, locking up funds at advantageous rates and times—in all these profit-making skills supercorporations will display their built-in superiority over most conventional corporations.

Although less likely, it is possible that some venture managers in the supers will sense ways of adding further to the ability of new cities to help their citizens ease their personal problems. After all, members of the conventional corporate community created Kaiser Industries' remarkably effective delivery system for medical care and developed teaching machines, are currently designing and producing pollution-control systems, and are supporting the successful training of hard-core unemployed through the New York Board of Trade and other business-sponsored organizations.

The remote possibility that supers will help in the social concerns of new cities originates in the supers' people-management programs that were probed in Part Two. The supercorporations, we said, not only will contribute quantitatively to people-management investments and experiments but will add vigor and subtlety. Thus, they may cause and also benefit from some advances in the management of interpersonal relationships. In this event, there is the further possibility that such discoveries could be translated into means for helping new-city residents deal with their own personal problems.

A more demonstrable point is that supercorporations will be able to form and manage complex partnerships and subventures. Way back in Part One, we looked at the evidence that conventional corporations' growth had been constricted by a series of "prudent" financial and operating policies. We saw that such policies were valid in concept but misapplied. It is impossible for a conventional corporation using such financial and operating policies in the traditional ways to start a new city. Almost every one of the prudent policies, conventionally applied, would by itself kill the contemplated sponsorship of a new city.

But we can see how less shackled companies have internally positioned themselves to lead and sponsor the tremendous new-city ventures. These indicators are early models for the supers' contributions to the new-city movement. Looking again at the Fox Valley East venture, we see immediately that it violates the conventional financial and operating precepts. No one owns 100 percent of the venture, as dogma would have required. We saw that there are five venture partners, whereas two was the typical number in the few joint ventures that the conventional corporations permitted themselves. The five partners represent a rich coverage of the capabilities necessary to maximize new-city success.

What more can supercorporations add? Several things—some different in nature, others different in degree. One is an appetite for acquisitions. A supercorporation can elect to own some of the specialized business enterprises needed for new-city development, expanding upon the example of Aetna's acquisition of Urban Investment and Development. This action would round up more of the scarce business talents and capabilities for new-city development and management.

Next, supercorporations would probably bring advanced systems approaches and technology to the planning, implementation, and operation of new cities. Few types of businesses can benefit more from a comprehensive systems approach than new cities. Of course, the systems approach can come up with negative results. General Electric devoted about two years and probably six-figure amounts of money to a systems approach that analyzed the new-city business as a potential venture. The results were negative, and GE told me in 1973 that it had no plan for going into new cities at all. GE's conclusion should be sobering for new-city enthusiasts. Among other salutary results, it should lead to additional systems modeling and other advanced investigations, so that the negatives that GE saw can best be met in the new cities that must be built.

Finally, in the mixed economy of the United States, it may be necessary for many of the new cities to be founded and operated with government aid and authority. If so, the extensive advantages of supercorporations in public-private partnerships and in the contract state would enable them to get more than their share of the new-city business and to handle it well. There is a fine art to successful government contracting, and few conventional corporations have mastered it. On this art alone, however, may hinge a good deal of the success or failure of our nationwide efforts to raise new cities.

Over 100 more new cities will add something like $100 billion to the assets of large U.S. corporations by 1990, and hopefully billions to their cash flows and after-tax profits. Within their boundaries, new cities will solve directly mechanical and/or social problems such as pollution and inadequate medical care. The new cities may even enable individuals to solve some of their personal problems through a more people-oriented environment. Supercorporations should get more than their share of the new-city business, and should usually succeed at it, although there will doubtless be some false starts and failures.

New cities are one of the most natural ventures for the special capabilities of supercorporations. They will bring needed strength in financing and financial management, for one of history's most expensive new products; venture management, for one of the more complex types of ventures of our era; advanced systems approaches and technology, as the complicated new-city business may require; and government contracting of the highest order, honed in other public-private partnerships and in ventures in the contract state.

Supercorporate sponsorship of new cities should also satisfy the objections of some of the opponents of corporate investments in our social concerns, thus partially clearing up a costly confusion in our society. New cities can be *both* profitable enterprises and powerful vehicles for dealing with an inclusive range of our most urgent social perils.

Epilogue

A BACKWARD LOOK at the FUTURE

YOU AND I have just taken a tour of the horizon over which I claim the new supercorporations are about to appear. We have considered the difficult postindustrial society, which seems to be post-everything we thought we understood. I addressed the leaden prospects of that society within the framework of the microfuture of business corporations. From the bottom up and from the inside of the corporate world toward the outside we have seen developments that may alter the big picture, the macrofuture.

This approach has led us, to name a few, into behaviorists' thoughts, Arab gold, intermediate technology, the contract state, multiple captives, new cities. Also you have been exposed to more than 40 predictions that are entwined with the notion of supercorporations.

I have tried to alarm you with some of these predictions. The great, new, postindustrial corporations, of which I see so much evidence, will be superaggressive, like ITT. Whether the force of a dozen more ITTs will be used for better or for worse depends as much on you as on the supers, semisupers, and their emulators.

Consider just once more the swinging conglomerates of the 1960s. To me, they are child's play compared with the new supercorporations. Yet those corporate adolescents turned and twisted millions of Americans and billions of dollars. Had we had an inkling of the deceit and disappointment ahead, who believes that these shenanigans could have been palmed off on us? A forewarning could have prevented our enchantment with those fallen corporate charmers.

Whether or not it gives you comfort, a few of my predictions are being confirmed right now. These are minor, but they are bound up in the basic predictions of the coming of the supercorporations. For instance, the price-fixing of professional fee schedules is already being attacked. Large-scale systems approaches to the problems of some Arab societies are now being formulated, while their incredible stores of currencies, as predicted, are being recycled into investments in many parts of the world. Private antitrust suits in this country are increasing, as are European antitrust moves. More multiple captives are being created, and still more are being planned. The extreme diversification of conventional corporations is continuing and apparently expanding. Conventional corporations are also continuing, if not accelerating, their acquisitions, divestments, joint ventures, and more elaborate financial structures and techniques. Thus, it may get harder to dismiss lightly this comprehensive set of predictions.

I hope that you will ruminate about the idea of supercorporations. If you can conceive that they might—just might—actually emerge in force, then you will leap to the next point: what to do about them. You now have the advantages of this book's early warning; the ball is in your court.

INDEX